Church History 101

An Introduction for Presbyterians

William M. Ramsay

GENEVA

Geneva Press
Louisville, Kentucky

Book design by Sharon Adams
Cover design by Mark Abrams

First edition
Published by Geneva Press
Louisville, Kentucky

This book is printed on acid-free paper that meets the American National Standards Institute Z39.48 standard. ∞

PRINTED IN THE UNITED STATES OF AMERICA

05 06 07 08 09 10 11 12 13 14—10 9 8 7 6 5 4 3 2 1

Library of Congress Cataloging-in-Publication Data

Ramsay, William M.
  Church history 101 : an introduction for Presbyterians / William M. Ramsay.—1st ed.
      p. cm.
  Includes bibliographical references.
  ISBN 0-664-50277-6 (alk. paper)
  1. Presbyterian Church—History.   2. Presbyterian Church—United States—History.
  3. Church history.   I. Title: Church history one hundred one.   II. Title: Church history one hundred and one.   III. Title.

  BX8931.3.R36   2005
  270—dc22   2004052381

For my grandsons,
Will, Daniel, Rhett, and Austin Ramsay,
with trust that they will have a share in continuing the story

Contents

Foreword   vii

1   The First Century (c. AD 30–100)   1

2   Martyrdom and "Victory" (c. 100–400)   10

3   Monks, Missionaries, and Other Saints (c. 400–1100)   24

4   Crusades, Colleges, and Cathedrals (c. 1100–1500)   37

5   The Reformation on the Continent (c. 1500–1700)   51

6   The Reformation in Great Britain (c. 1500–1700)   66

7   The Church Comes to America (c. 1500–1800)   81

8   American Churches in Recent Centuries (c. 1800–Present)   98

9   Presbyterians in America (c. 1650–Present)   117

Appendix   137

Notes   140

Foreword

*T*he Bible tells a story, the story of the people of God. It begins with God and the first man and woman. It tells how God called Sarah and Abraham, how God rescued the chosen people from Egypt, how they sinned, how prophets warned them, how they were taken captive to Babylon, and how God restored them. The climax is the story of Jesus.

The story, however, does not end there. Acts continues it, telling how the church began to spread the gospel, was persecuted, and shared with those in need.

But then Acts breaks off. There is Paul under house arrest for two years. But what happened then? Did God stop doing mighty acts for and though God's people? Did they stop sinning and being judged and repenting and being restored? Were there no more prophetic leaders and heroic martyrs? No, God continued to work with and through the church. The story continues, warning us but also encouraging and inspiring us. Yet so many people do not know this story, our story. This book is to help individuals and study groups to hear that story anew.

Special thanks go to several people. Years ago the late Dr. Aubrey Brown asked me to write a weekly commentary on Dr. Ernest Trice Thompson's *Through the Ages* for *The Presbyterian Outlook*. Dr. Robert Bullock, a later editor of that excellent publication, graciously gave me permission to make free use of those articles. I am grateful to the Rev. Dr. Peter Hobbie, church historian and professor of religion at Presbyterian College, Clinton, S.C., and to Dr. Ernest Hooper, for many years a professor of history at Middle Tennessee State University, for reading the manuscript and making many suggestions for improving it. Bethel, the College of the Cumberland Presbyterian Church, McKenzie, Tennessee, let me teach some of these things there. Claudette Pickle and Davis Grey of the Cumberland Presbyterians' denominational center in

Memphis have encouraged me to think this book will be helpful to Cumberland Presbyterians as well as those for whom it is primarily intended, lay study groups in the Presbyterian Church (U.S.A.).

Of course the greatest help in more ways than I can count has been my wife, DeVere Maxwell Ramsay.

William M. Ramsay
April 23, 2004

Chapter 1

The First Century
(c. AD 30–100)

*E*mperor Nero had a problem. In AD 64 Rome had burned. Moreover, whether true or false, rumors were circulating around the city that Nero himself had started that fire. He needed someone to blame, so he decided on the perfect scapegoat: the Christians. After all, the pagan historian Tacitus tells us, they were everywhere "hated for their abominations." The Christians' leader, Christus, he tells us, had been executed under Procurator Pontius Pilate.

> Checked for the moment, this pernicious superstition again broke out. . . . Accordingly, arrest was first made of those who confessed [sc. to being Christians]; then, on their evidence, an immense multitude was convicted. . . . They were made to serve as objects of amusement; they were clad in the hides of beasts and torn to death by dogs; others were crucified, others set on fire. . . . All this gave rise to a feeling of pity, even towards men whose guilt merited the most exemplary punishment; for it was felt that they were being destroyed . . . to gratify the cruelty of an individual.[1]

Tradition says that Peter and Paul were among those who perished in that persecution. Outside the New Testament itself, that story is our first clear account of the early Christian church.

The Church in Acts—Luke's Picture of an Ideal Church

Within the New Testament, the book of Acts sets out to tell the story of the infant church. Writing perhaps around AD 80, Luke describes the first congregation in ideal terms. He pictures the Jerusalem church as a charismatic fellowship so loving that they shared everything they possessed. For example,

1

Barnabas gave all he owned into the church's funds. Peter and John were able to perform miracles of healing; Peter even raised the dead! They were repeatedly filled with the Spirit. Good Jews, they worshiped regularly in the temple. Jesus had appointed apostles, and these became their leaders. They preached that the Messiah had come, had been crucified, had risen from the dead, and was coming again, probably quite soon. According to Luke, thousands were quickly won to their fellowship and received baptism. Persecution, climaxed by the martyrdom of Stephen, forced them to disperse, but it could not stop their witness. As they scattered they continued to make converts. Among those were people of different races. Legends say Thomas took the gospel to India, and Mark to Egypt.

Paul (Saul) himself had been involved in the persecution that led to the martyrdom of Stephen. Luke so focuses the latter half of Acts on the mission of this one man, his hero, that we miss learning about many other things that we would like to know. The gospel had already reached Rome before Paul arrived there, Luke notes, but he never tells us how that church was begun. He says nothing of how the church came to Damascus or Egypt. He does tell us how Paul and some of his partner missionaries went from one major city to another in what is now Turkey and in Greece, making converts everywhere.

The typical church established by Paul was, Luke tells us, an outgrowth of the synagogue. Jews were scattered over the Roman world, and in first-century Judaism became, briefly, in some sense a missionary religion (Matt. 28:15). Many Gentiles were attracted by the monotheism and the high moral standards of the Jews. Some even underwent circumcision and became Jewish proselytes; others (called in Acts "God-fearers") attended the synagogue but were not actually enrolled. It was among these Gentiles that Paul had his greatest success. One may guess that that was true also of other traveling evangelists. Paul welcomed all races without requiring the circumcision that was essential in the Jewish law.

Inevitably this easing of the law produced friction. Synagogues split. Many Jewish Christians were distressed that Paul seemed to be abandoning the true Mosaic faith. Not only non-Christian Jews but also Jewish converts to Christianity attacked Paul verbally and sometimes physically. He was at times forced to flee, leaving behind a young church to face the opposition. Nothing, however, could stop him or dismay his followers. At least according to Acts, after considerable dispute the church agreed to accept uncircumcised Gentiles. A formal assembly of apostles and elders considered the matter, and James, the brother of Jesus, announced the consensus: all races, circumcised and uncircumcised, were to be welcomed.

The Church in Corinth—A Contentious Group
of Sinners "Saved by Grace"

No doubt Luke is quite honest in his description. He was writing, however, to present the church in the best possible light. Paul's two letters to the church at Corinth reveal a somewhat more realistic picture of an early congregation.

If you had visited the church at Corinth you would have found it torn by factions. Its members tended to split into parties based on loyalty to different preachers, each party thinking itself superior to the others. Though Paul had founded the church, after his departure you might hear rivals attacking his reputation. They would tell you that he was not true to the law, that he was a poor preacher, and that his real motivations were self-glory and money. They, on the other hand, claimed to be better Jews and to be far wiser and more knowledgeable than Paul.

If you became a member you would often share a meal with the others. Sometimes it was disorderly. You would notice that the rich tended to go ahead and eat, not waiting to share with the poor slaves and other laborers who could not come until they got off work. Sometimes people even got drunk at the Lord's Supper. Paul's corrections and instructions to them in 1 Corinthians 11 were to become guidelines for the church through the ages.

Their worship might sometimes seem to you to be a disorderly confusion. Apparently any member might speak when he or she felt moved by the Spirit; often several spoke at once. Speaking with tongues, pictured in Acts as communication across language barriers, might appear to you to be meaningless babble. Interpreting what a tongues speaker had said was often part of the worship, but too often that was neglected. Paul had to plead for order.

One of the things that would startle you would be the freedom of the Christian women. As we will see from other parts of the New Testament, in the earliest days women were often leaders in the church. In Corinth women tended to speak aloud in church just as did the men. Apparently some newly "liberated" women even talked back to or disobeyed their husbands. Some women's dress and hairstyles might have shocked you; much of the conduct of the women offended Paul.

Not all the members of the church would have seemed to you models of morality. One man was living in incest. Another was suing a fellow church member. Paul had to remind the congregation of even the most elementary kind of sexual morality.

Nevertheless, you would have been deeply attracted to this church. These "saints" were not perfect, but they were bound together in many ways. Behind the apparent disorder you would discern some beginnings of organization. There were members with identifiable gifts and responsibilities: teachers, healers, servants to people in need. Masters and slaves ate at the same table. They shared in courage as they faced the difficulties and disciplines their new faith involved. They lived in hope of eternal life, already being given them by Christ. To enter that fellowship you would be baptized, a mystical, transforming experience. The Holy Spirit, though sometimes manifest in ways that would seem strange to you, gave church members a genuine sense of joy, of kinship, of peace, and even a quite remarkable love. They told and retold you the story of how Jesus was the Savior of the world, how he died for you, how he had risen from the dead and thus conquered death, and how he would be manifest in glorious victory in the end. You would begin to join them in doing deeds of mercy. You would know yourself to be a sinner, but a sinner saved by grace. With your new brothers and sisters you would know yourself to be bound in love, together members of the mystical body of Christ.

The Church in Some Other New Testament Books

Matthew 10 gives us some insight into the practice of some others of the first evangelists. Originally in Palestine, but soon almost anywhere in the empire, you might have been visited by a traveling preacher. Feeling that he—perhaps sometimes she—could rely entirely on God, and following directions said to have been laid down by Jesus, he would arrive penniless and without even a change of clothes. Many would listen to his announcement that the Messiah had come, had been crucified, had risen from the dead, and was to return soon. Excited by this news, some family would often provide hospitality for the stranger, and he would voice a blessing on that household. He would not stay long, however. Instead he would hurry on to the next town, wanting to reach as many people as possible with the news before the Messiah came again. Not every community welcomed such an evangelist. Religious and governmental authorities might regard him as a challenge to their leadership. He would respond with a solemn curse and hurry on down the road.[2]

As a church developed, Matthew 16 suggests, its leaders would indeed claim authority, though they sought to exercise discipline gently. If, for example, it was discovered that a church member was delinquent in attending worship or was suspected of adultery, a member of the church would visit him privately. If that failed to bring repentance, two or three more would try to persuade him to repent. If even that did not succeed, his case would be discussed publicly by the church. If he continued unrepentant he would be barred from the Lord's Supper. With the gospel and the Lord's Supper, the church felt that it had the keys by which it opened the door into the kingdom; but sometimes through excommunication it might have to lock that door on the faithless. But the door was always open to the truly penitent.[3]

It is surprising that in the male-dominated society of the first-century Roman Empire Paul could write that in the church "there is no longer . . . male and female; for you are all one in Christ Jesus." Though men were soon protesting, in the beginning women were often the leaders in the church. The Gospels name a number of women who during Jesus' earthly life accompanied him and provided the money that enabled him to devote his time exclusively to his ministry of teaching and healing. As the church spread, women of some wealth, such as Lydia and Chloe, must have provided meeting places and financial support for the church's ministry, and would have exercised the influence that such generosity brings. The Gospels' stories of Easter seem to differ from one another in many details, but on one thing they agree: the first witnesses to Jesus' resurrection were women. It was women who first brought the good news to men. The repetition of that report probably reflects something more than just the memory of that one Sunday morning. Paul names Junia as an "apostle," in fact a prominent one.[4] Paul names Priscilla, Euodia, Syntyche, and others as leaders who worked in partnership with him. Phoebe held the office of deacon. Acts speaks of Phillip's daughters as recognized "prophets."

Few things the early church did were to have more impact on subsequent generations than this: by the end of the first century stories and sayings of Jesus had been collected and our four Gospels had been written. Some letters of Paul, too, were widely known. Indeed, all the books that were later to make up our New Testament were written in the first century or very soon thereafter. The books were not yet all collected, selected, and canonized, however.

The Church in the Pastoral Epistles

Though from the time of Nero persecution may always have been a possibility, there is little evidence of it in 1 and 2 Timothy and Titus. Often called "the Pastoral Epistles," they come to us as letters of Paul. It is widely held, however, that at least in the form we now have them they give us pictures of the church from a time somewhat later than that of the apostle, or even of Matthew, cited above. They are often dated around AD 90 or even later. The church was changing.

Heresy is spreading, false teaching masquerading as the gospel. A special concern of these letters is that the gospel be taught and preserved in its original purity. One way of achieving this goal is by the use of "sound words," little creeds. Here is one you might have learned if you had been a member of one of these congregations:

there is one God;
   there is also one mediator between God and humankind,
Christ Jesus, himself human,
   who gave himself a ransom for all.

(1 Tim. 2:5–6)

Another way of protecting the gospel was through validated leadership. These letters seem to assume that the church has an organizational pattern. Timothy appears to be the installed pastor of a congregation. He has been gifted with this office through a ceremony of laying on of hands by a council of elders ("presbytery" in the King James Version). (The word "Presbyterian" comes from the Greek word for "elder.") The congregation must respect Timothy as pastor even though he is young. He is to give attention especially "to the public reading of scripture, to exhorting, to teaching" (1 Tim. 4:13). The Scriptures he reads will help guard against heresy. They were to be taught by approved teachers; all were to study them. (At this stage, of course, "the scriptures" were the Jewish Scriptures, the Old Testament.)

There are also officers called "bishops" (overseers), who seem to be the same as "elders." Apparently there are several in each church. These elders rule the church, and some preach and teach. There are also "deacons" (servants). We are told that they must be people of blameless character, but unfortunately we are not told what their duties are.

One "problem" is women who, as church members, like those earlier women mentioned in 1 Corinthians, seem to be claiming the right to speak in church even as do men. Some have become teachers and occupy positions of authority. If Timothy follows the practice of the writer of these epistles, however, those women will be silenced. They also must be forbidden to dress with the braided hairstyles of the day or to wear jewelry.

There is, however, a special group of women: enrolled widows. The writer lays down careful restrictions about which women may be included on this list, but the old women who qualify merit support and honor by the church. They are to spend much time in prayers, "night and day." They are perhaps the spiritual ancestors of the sisterhoods that came into being in subsequent centuries.

Of course the worship in the congregation included much prayer, prayers of thanksgiving and intercession for all. These Christians even interceded for their civil rulers, some of whom had already begun to persecute Christians.

Men prayed aloud, hands held high in the traditional Jewish manner, though the writer wants women to remain silent.

If then, about AD 90, you had worshiped in a Christian congregation, you would have heard a reading from the Old Testament. An approved pastor would preach a sermon exhorting you to faithfulness and moral living. You might have joined in reciting or singing a creed. You would have prayed as men in the congregation raised their hands and prayed aloud. In some congregations, however, if you were a woman and tried to pray aloud too, or your dress or hairstyle had seemed immodest, you might have been warned that you were violating the rules. The man giving that warning might be called an "elder."

The Church in Revelation

In the first letter that bears the name of Peter, the author refers to himself as an elder. He, however, finds it necessary to warn his readers not about rules but that a "fiery ordeal" is about to come upon them. The relatively peaceful times of the Pastoral Epistles were not going to last.

At least in parts of what is now Turkey, the mid-90s were indeed a time of testing, and by no means all the members of the infant church remained faithful. It had never been easy to be a Christian. If you were a building contractor or a common laborer you could no longer work on a pagan temple. If you were a sculptor you had to reject offers to make idols. Some questioned whether one could have a Christian's love for enemies and still serve in the army. Pagan temples were the butcher shops of the ancient world, so that as a Christian housewife you might have to make your family become vegetarians or else seem to share in pagan sacrifices. Christians might be reluctant to go to parties at pagan temples or eat at a dinner party food from temple shops. Thus they offended friends and even made enemies. Most especially if confronted with the choice of conforming to emperor worship or facing imprisonment and even death, a Christian might be tempted to renounce the faith. Many compromised or even gave up on being Christians. The book of Revelation was written as a plea to church members to remain true even if faithfulness meant martyrdom.

After his death Roman historians described the emperor Domitian as a cruel monster who had friends and family members assassinated if they displeased him and who entertained himself by sticking pins through insects. Christian tradition called him another Nero and charged him with widespread slaughter of Christians. In more recent years historians have defended Domitian as in many ways a just and concerned ruler and have argued that there is little evidence of an effort to stamp out the church during his reign. The book of Revelation, they propose, describes a persecution John's apocalyptic vision simply anticipates, not one already in progress. The truth probably lies between these two views. In the 50s Paul could affirm that the governing authorities were ordained by God. In the 90s John sees them as agents of Satan. Surely the relationship of Rome to the church must have changed. Domitian certainly did like to head his decrees, "Domitian, Lord and God." The cult of emperor worship was strong in what is now Turkey, the area of the churches to which the Apocalypse is addressed. Formal recognition of the emperor's divinity was a patriotic duty. The author of Revelation is in Patmos, probably exiled for his preaching. He names one martyr in Pergamum, Antipas, killed for his faithfulness. Repeatedly John pictures many martyrs in heaven, and he describes Rome as drenched with the blood of the saints. At the very least it would seem that the situation is like what we know existed by AD 112, some fifteen or twenty years after John wrote. Then, as we will see in the next chapter, if an enemy, perhaps a competitor, reported that some neighbor was a Christian, as enemies often did, and if that Christian then refused to engage in a brief ceremonial worship of the emperor, prison and even death would follow.

Thus, in the reign of Domitian, John commends the churches at Ephesus and Thyatira for their "patient endurance." He pleads with the church at Smyrna to be "faithful unto death." However, the third-generation church at Ephesus has "abandoned the love" they had at first. The church at Sardis seems dead, and the faith of the church at Laodicea is only lukewarm.

"Beware," John warns, "the devil is about to throw some of you into prison so that you may be tested, and . . . you will have affliction." But John says that Christ couples that warning with a promise: "Be faithful until death, and I will give you a crown of life" (Rev. 2:10).

As a matter of fact, repeatedly in the next two centuries that testing was to come.

Questions Chapter 1

1. The New Testament begins with a brief summary of the Old Testament (Matt. 1:1–7). In what sense is the New Testament a continuation of the story told in the Old Testament? In what sense, if any, does the history of the church seem to you a continuation of the New Testament's story?
2. Acts 2:41–47 gives a brief picture of the ideal church. Look at it phrase by phrase and consider how your congregation's nature and program compare with it.

3. Here are some verses that suggest that the church in Corinth was less than ideal: 1 Cor. 1:10–12; 5:1; 11:17–21; and 14:26–33a. In what ways is the church today like the church in Corinth? How is it dealing with its problems?
4. In what ways does Presbyterian Church government reflect the principles implied in the following verses: 1 Tim. 3:1–8; 4:14; Titus 1:5–7; Acts 15:6–7?
5. What can you infer about the place of women in the earliest church from such verses as Matt. 28:10; Acts 16:13–15; Rom. 16:3–16; and Phil. 4:2–3? What is implied by later efforts to forbid women to speak or to have any authority, as suggested by 1 Tim. 2:11–12?
6. What can you tell about worship in a first-century church from these verses: 1 Tim. 2:1–2; 4:6, 13; 6:11; 2 Tim. 2:11–13? How is Presbyterian worship now like worship then?

Chapter 2

Martyrdom and "Victory" (c. 100–400)

*B*eginning with the earthly life of Jesus himself, for some three hundred years it was never quite safe to be a Christian. Christians did not worship the familiar gods; some Christians refused to serve in the army; and some even refused to participate in a perfunctory recognition of the divinity of the emperor. To many of the emperor's subjects this seemed subversive, far more unpatriotic than refusing to salute the flag or sing "The Star Spangled Banner" would seem in the United States. Probably because of the high place Christians gave women, rumors circulated that they secretly engaged in free love. The baptism of infants and the eating of Christ's body at the Lord's Supper in a ceremony closely restricted to church members gave rise to rumors of infanticide and cannibalism. In one way we can be glad for such attacks on the church: they prompted a number of Christians to write to defend the church and thus gave us vivid descriptions of what second-century Christians and congregations were like.

The Life and Worship of Christians in the Second Century

Early in the second century an unknown writer defended Christians by describing how they actually lived:

> They marry like all other men and they beget children; but they do not cast away their offspring. . . . They have their meals in common, but not their wives. . . . They obey the established laws, and they surpass the laws in their own lives. They love all men, and they are persecuted by all. . . . They are reviled, and they bless; they are insulted, and they respect. Doing good they are punished as evil-doers; being punished they rejoice, as if they were thereby quickened by life. . . . Christians when punished increase more and more daily.[1]

Indeed, the writer argued, the church is to the empire what the soul is to the body. Scattered through the empire, the world hates them as the flesh hates the spirit. It is Christians, however, the writer boasts, who hold the world together and give it life.

By the middle of the second century at least one philosopher, Justin, who by his heroic death was later to earn the title "Justin Martyr," was defending Christian beliefs to his fellow intellectuals. He argued that the teachings of Christianity were not bizarre, as enemies charged. They were in accordance with the *Logos* (Word or divine Reason) of which the wisest philosophers, Socrates and Plato, had spoken. Those true philosophers were, he claimed, forerunners of the Christian faith for the Greeks as the prophets had been for the Jews. Replying to charges that Christians in secret carried on horrible orgies, Justin described what actually went on in a typical Sunday morning service in a second-century congregation. Here, then, is what you might experience if you attended a worship service on a second-century Sunday.

> On the so-called day of the Sun there is a meeting of all of us . . . and the memoirs of the Apostles or the writings of the prophets are read, as long as time allows. Then . . . the president gives by word of mouth his admonition and exhortation to follow these excellent things. Afterwards we all rise at once and offer prayers; and . . . when we have ceased to pray, bread is brought and wine and water, and the president likewise offers up prayers and thanksgiving to the best of his power and the people responds with its Amen. Then follows the distribution to each and the partaking of that for which thanks were given; and to them that are absent a portion is sent by the hand of the deacons. Of those that are well to do and willing, every one gives what he will according to his own purpose, and the collection is deposited with the president, and he it is that succours orphans and widows, and those that are in want through sickness or any other cause, and those that are in bonds and the strangers that are sojourning, and in short he has the care of all that are in need.[2]

Justin's account defending this typical worship service was needed. At any moment the peaceful fellowship he described might be invaded by the Roman police.

Persecution in the Second Century

Only a few of the Roman emperors sought out Christians and tried everywhere to stamp out the church. Paradoxically, it was usually the best emperors, those who worked hardest to unify the empire, who were the most concerned to get rid of Christianity. Even under the most lax rulers, however, until the imperial decrees of AD 311 and 313, Christians were never really out of danger.

The problem was that the state and religion were closely entwined. Any failure to reverence the emperor and the traditional Roman gods seemed a threat to the state. The emperor's efforts to unite the empire through religion ran into the stone walls of Christianity and Judaism. Most officials did not care what people in their districts worshiped. Some Christian's neighbor, however, might be offended by what seemed bizarre and unpatriotic behavior, or a competitor might become jealous of a successful Christian rival. That neighbor might accuse a Christian to the authorities, and that accusation might force an official to act.

About AD 112 Pliny, a Roman governor in what is now Turkey, wrote the emperor Trajan for advice in such a situation:

> I have hesitated a great deal on the question whether there should be any distinction of ages; whether the weak should have the same treatment as the more robust; whether these who recant should be pardoned, or whether a man who has ever been a Christian should gain nothing by ceasing to be such, whether the name itself, even if innocent of crime, should be punished, or only the crimes attaching to that name.
>
> Meanwhile, this is the course that I have adopted in the case of those brought before me as Christians. I ask them if they are Christians. If they admit it I repeat the question a second and a third time, threatening capital punishment; if they persist I sentence them to death. For I do not doubt that, whatever kind of crime it may be to which they have confessed, their pertinacity and inflexible obstinacy should certainly be punished. . . .
>
> Any who denied that they were or had been Christians I considered should be discharged, because they called upon the gods at my dictation and did reverence, with incense and wine, to your image . . . especially because they cursed Christ, a thing which, it is said, genuine Christians cannot be induced to do.[3]

The emperor assured the governor that he was doing the right thing. Anybody who denied being a Christian and showed it by doing reverence to the gods should be regarded as innocent, however likely it was that he or she had been a Christian in the past.

Apparently it was easy to avoid persecution. Just do a quick ceremony of reverence to the gods, and you could go free. Many, of course, availed themselves of that simple escape, but there were also many who because of what Pliny called their "inflexible obstinacy" refused. The church called that "obstinacy" faithfulness.

Our earliest Christian writings after the New Testament include letters written about AD 112 by a bishop named Ignatius. (A lovely but probably groundless legend says that he had been the child whom Jesus took in his arms, blessed, and set in the midst of the crowd.) Now an old man, he had been arrested, and like Paul half a century earlier, was being taken to Rome on his way to his death. Christians there, however, knowing that he was coming, devised a plot to help him escape. Hearing of their plan he wrote a letter dissuading them from the rescue. He wanted to give his life for his Lord, meeting the full test of being a Christian in a time of persecution.

Emperor Marcus Aurelius wrote essays in Stoic philosophy that are still treasured, and he was an enlightened ruler. He was, however, superstitious. The empire was suffering from floods, invasions, and other difficulties, and seers told him that one cause was the Christians. He clamped down on them. Among those who died as a result was Justin Martyr, part of whose defense of the church was quoted above.

Ever since that era Christians have been inspired by the story of the death of the aged Polycarp, bishop of Smyrna. Since he would not worship the ancestral gods, he was accused of atheism. When the soldiers came for him he invited them first to have dinner, then went with them peacefully to the stadium where a crowd had gathered to watch his execution. "Say, 'Away with the atheists!'" the authorities demanded. He agreed; waving his hand at the bloodthirsty mob, he cried, "Away with the atheists!" That did not satisfy the proconsul. "Swear by the genus [the divine authority] of Caesar," he ordered. Polycarp refused, even when the proconsul threatened to throw him to wild beasts. Instead he gave his testimony to Christ, "Eighty and six years have I served him, and he hath done me no wrong; how then can I blaspheme my king who saved me?" They burned him to death.

Almost from the first, being a Christian was against the law, a law sometimes ignored but sometimes vigorously enforced. Here and there persecution might break out. Sanctus, placed on trial, refused to give his name. He would reply to every question with only one sentence, "I am a Christian."

Rome's Effort to Destroy the Church

The first systematic empire-wide persecution designed to stamp out the church was in AD 202. Being emperor was not an easy job. Septimus Severus found himself ruler of a vast area with many different languages, cultures, loyalties, and cults. One thing might unite the diverse empire, he reasoned, a unifying faith. Let every group keep its own religion and every cult its own practices, but let all of them also acknowledge as supreme over all other gods the Unconquered Sun. Many Jews and Christians refused. To stop the spread of these rebellious religions the emperor decreed that anyone converting to them would be executed.

Among the martyrs of this persecution whose stories the church treasured was that of Perpetua and her four associates. They were catechumens preparing for baptism. Some may have been teenagers. Perpetua was a young, wealthy woman, a new mother. Her father and others tried to persuade her to renounce her faith. The conclusion of the trial was delayed in hopes that she would recant, but she stood firm. Her slave Felicitas was pregnant. As she groaned in giving birth, they asked her how she would face the even worse terrors of the wild beasts in the arena. "Now my sufferings are only mine," she replied. "But when I face the beasts there will be another who will live in me, and will suffer for me since I shall be suffering for him."[4] Brought before the crowd in the arena, first the three men were killed by wild beasts. Perpetua and Felicitas were then attacked by a ferocious cow. Perpetua asked to be allowed to retie her hair, for loose hair was a sign of mourning and she considered her martyrdom a time of joy. Bruised and bleeding, at last the young women were executed by the sword. A Christian woman adopted Felicitas's baby.

That persecution subsided. By AD 250, however, the emperor Decius faced multiple problems: Persians on the east, Goths on the north, economic depression, and a plague sweeping across the empire. The biggest problem, he felt, was that Rome had lost its ancient spirit, nourished by its ancient faith. Rome needed a revival of "true" religion; he would bring it about by force. He appointed a day, therefore, on which all his subjects would be required to sacrifice to the ancestral gods. They would sign the following statement: "I have always sacrificed to the gods, and now in your presence, in accordance with the terms of the edict, I have done sacrifice and poured libations and tasted the sacrifices, and I request you to certify to this effect. Farewell."[5] A magistrate would attest the certificate. Some Christians recanted their faith. Others sought in various ways to evade the edict, which was not always carefully enforced. Corrupt officials might sell certificates to Christians who had never actually given in. Many, however, faced confiscation of property, exile, torture, and even death. Fortunately for the church, Decius's reign ended a year later. Six years later the emperor Valerian renewed the persecution, but he was soon captured by the Persians. The next emperor restored property to the Christians and church buildings to the church. For the next four decades the church had relative peace.

What sparked the last and most violent persecution of Christians was a disturbance related to the army. It had long been true that while some Christians had served in the army, many church leaders had protested that Christians could not love their enemies and turn the other cheek to them while attacking them with spears and swords. Some Christians attempted to leave the army and others refused to become soldiers.

The conflict grew. In February 303, Diocletian issued a decree that all churches would be destroyed, all copies of the Scriptures would be burned, all Christians of high rank would lose their citizenship, and all others would be reduced to slavery. Two fires broke out in the palace, and, as in the days of Nero, they were blamed on the Christians. Prisons filled and stayed full even though pardon was offered those who would recant. One observer records a pitiful march of nearly one hundred Christian men, women, and children, all with their right eye put out and their left foot crippled, on their way to slavery in the mines.

All copies of the Scriptures were to be destroyed. The word "traitor" may have originated with those who traded gospels in exchange for their lives. One officer demanded that a prisoner read him something from the banned book. "Blessed are they who are persecuted for righteousness' sake, for theirs in the kingdom of heaven," the Christian read from Matthew.

The early church historian Eusebius tells how a soldier named Marinus was about to be promoted. A rival protested that Marinus was a Christian. After examination the judge gave Marinus three hours in which to repent. Taking him to the church, his bishop pulled aside his robe and disclosed a copy of the Gospels and a sword. He must choose one or the other, the bishop said. He chose the Bible. "Hold fast, then, hold fast to God, and strengthened by him, mayest thou obtain what thou hast chosen—go in peace." Marinus was beheaded, or, as Eusebius put it, was "made perfect by martyrdom."[6]

Eusebius tells us that in Egypt alone, "Thousands, both men, and women, and children, despising the present life for the sake of our Saviour's doctrine, submitted to death in various shapes. Some, after being tortured with scrapings and the rack, and the most dreadful scourgings . . . were finally committed to the flames. . . . Some . . . were nailed with the head downwards, and kept alive until they were destroyed by starving on the cross itself."[7]

The Greek word *martyros* means "witness." In spite of the danger of martyrdom and often inspired by that witness, more and more people became Christians. The second-century theologian Tertullian had written rightly that the blood of the martyrs is the seed of the church. Early in the fourth century a kind of "victory" would come.

"Victory" (?)

"Sing to the Lord a new song, because he hath done wonderful works. His right hand hath saved him, and his holy right arm." So Eusebius exulted.

"Now a bright and splendid day, with no overshadowing cloud, irradiated the churches in the whole world with its celestial light."[8] "All who before were sunk in sorrow, beheld each other with smiling and cheerful faces. With choirs and hymns, in the cities and villages, at the same time they celebrated and extolled first of all God the universal King . . . then they also celebrated the praises of the pious emperor."[9] The cause of the jubilation was this: Constantine, who called himself a Christian, had become emperor. The persecution was ended. To Eusebius and thousands of other Christians it must have seemed that in its battle with the empire the church had won.

Many Eastern Orthodox Christians still call him *Saint* Constantine. Just how saintly he was can be debated. He could rival his predecessors in cruelty to his enemies. For some years after professing to be a Christian he continued to participate in services of worship to the Unconquered Sun. Like many others in his day, he delayed baptism until he was near death so that his whole life's sins might be washed away. Nevertheless, he affirmed that he had indeed been converted. He is said to have cried that if only he could have been at the cross with a legion of his soldiers he would have rescued his Lord. He was certainly a friend and patron of the church.

In the year 312 he defeated his rival and seized power in the western part of the empire. According to a credible legend, the night before that battle at Milvian Bridge he had a dream in which he saw a cross in the heavens and the words, "In this sign conquer." He did conquer. On his military standards he placed the monogram *chi rho*, the first two letters of the Greek word *Christos*. In 311 the emperor Galerius, on his deathbed from a disease he believed was a punishment from God, had decreed pardon to all Christians and toleration for their faith. In 313 Constantine's Edict of Milan guaranteed that that freedom would continue. Soon Constantine was to make Christianity the state religion. Eventually the persecuted would become the persecutors.

State support brought many good things. To most Christians the best of these was that they no longer had to fear persecution because of their faith. Favor by the state encouraged rapid growth for the church. At the time of Constantine's conversion perhaps 1 in 20—some even estimate 1 in 10—had become Christians. A century later most people in the Mediterranean world were at least nominally Christians.

The oldest church building archaeologists have discovered was in Dura in Syria and dates from about AD 235. Now great buildings could be built, often at government expense. The first St. Peter's Church in Rome was begun on the site of what was thought to be Peter's grave. In Palestine a church was built on the traditional site of Jesus' sepulcher and another in Bethlehem where Jesus was born. Church buildings appeared all over the empire.

New humane laws relieved suffering. Before Constantine it was legal for a father to sell a child into slavery or to kill it. Now this became a crime. Earlier, divorce was so common that Seneca could joke of one Maecenas that he "married a thousand times." Caius Gallus divorced his wife because he saw her walking in the street bareheaded. Husbands owned all property. Constantine, however, began new regulations on divorce, made it illegal for a married man to have concubines, and protected the wife's property rights. Prisons were reformed. Hospitals were established.

Dangers and Protests

Some have said that "the devil joined the church when Constantine became a Christian." A symbol of the times is a Roman coin showing a deity, divine Lord Mithra, but now holding in his hand a cross.

Some compromises with the culture may seem harmless. December 25 was a festival celebrating the birth of the sun god. Christians baptized it as Christmas, celebrating the birth of Jesus. Other mergers with popular custom were more questionable. Protests against participation in war virtually disappeared. Once the church had questioned how a rich man could enter the kingdom of heaven. Now the church itself gloried in its wealth. Pomp and ceremony, modeled in part on that of the state, replaced the simpler worship of the early church. Allied with a hierarchical, dictatorial government, the church gave more and more authority to its own hierarchy, with laypeople having a smaller role in the worship and the government of the church. Indeed, the emperor himself issued decrees concerning church government and doctrine.

The most dangerous compromise, however, lay in the church's growing worldliness. As Søren Kierkegaard was to warn many centuries later, when everybody is a Christian, nobody is a Christian. Once the threat of persecution had weeded out all but the truly committed Christians. Now awareness of the tension between the kingdom of this world and the kingdom of God was fading. Once the lives of candidates for church membership were examined for months before they could be baptized. Soon every subject was expected by law to become a church member.

At least from the third century on there were holy men and women who dramatically lived out their protest against worldliness. Anchorites retired to the desert to devote themselves to prayer, even seeking physical suffering to put down the flesh and thus exalt their souls. Ancient reports tell us stories about them. Macarius lay naked six months in a swamp, rejoicing as mosquitoes and poisonous insects stung him nearly to death. Sabrinus would eat only rotted corn. One "holy man" is said to have wept over the sins of the world until his eyelashes fell off. Having withdrawn from the sinful world to live on top of a column, Simeon Stylites refused to come down even for his own mother's funeral.

Yet when they felt needed to help the world, even some of these strange people might come back. Twice the great ascetic Anthony returned from the desert. Once it was to strengthen Christians in persecution. What could the Romans do to him that he had not already done to himself? He came back again to defend the faith against the Arian heresy.

Setting Standards for the Church: A Pattern of Government

Three things helped the church to remain united and to protect the gospel "once for all delivered to the saints": the church evolved a system of government, it canonized the Scriptures, and it developed authoritative creeds.

We know from Paul's letters to the church at Corinth that the early church could sometimes seem almost chaotic. Very early "prophets," professing to be inspired by the Holy Spirit, were announcing oracles of diverse kinds. To encourage order, by the middle of the second century someone wrote a manual of rules and regulations for the church. Called the *Didache,* or the *Teaching of the Twelve Apostles*, it specified that baptism should preferably be by immersion in running water, but if that was not readily available then still water or pouring were permissible. Hospitality should be given to traveling evangelists, but only for three days. If they stayed longer they should get a job and not drain the finances of the congregation. For what this little book called the Eucharist, there was a suggested prayer for the bread and a similar one for the wine.

Rule books alone, however, were not enough; the church evolved a system of government to see that the rules were followed. About AD 112 Ignatius, on his way to martyrdom in Rome, wrote that Christians must always be subject to their bishops. For example, how and when should one worship? Late in the second century Victor, bishop of Rome, excommunicated a whole group of churches. The sin for which he thus condemned them to hell was not adultery or murder; it was that they celebrated Easter on the wrong day. Fortunately other bishops talked him out of it. Though in the powerful position of presiding over the churches in the capital of the empire, the bishop of Rome was not yet acknowledged as the authority over all other bishops. (The infallibility of the pope was not declared essential doctrine until 1870.) But very early the authority of all bishops was growing. Some of the bishops claimed to be the successors of various apostles. The bishop of Rome claimed apostolic succession from Peter, leader of the apostles.

Presbyterian historian Ernest Trice Thompson used to tell his classes that, oversimplified, one might broadly describe the evolution of church government like this:

First century—several "bishops" or "elders" in each congregation.
Second century—one bishop over one congregation.
Third century—one bishop over several congregations.
Fourth century—some (metropolitan) bishops over other bishops.
Fifth century—one bishop (the bishop of Rome) exercising, or attempting to exercise, authority over all others.[10]

Citing Matthew 16:18 and evidence of the respect early leaders had for the bishops of Rome, many Roman Catholic historians would strongly disagree with that analysis.

Setting Standards for the Church: The Canonization of Scripture

From the very beginning the Christian church regarded the Jews' Scriptures as authoritative. When, about AD 51, Paul dictated his first letter to the church at Thessalonica, he had no idea that he was beginning a new canon (books that make up a rule of faith). He did, however, expect his letters to be read to the churches to which they were sent. 2 Peter 3:15–16 shows that quite early Paul's letters were being collected and circulated among the churches.

Luke 1:1–4 tells us that the author of that Gospel was familiar with various earlier accounts of the life of Christ. Some, we can tell from his Gospel, probably were written accounts: the Gospel of Mark, a collection of sayings of Jesus, and probably others. Quite early, fanciful stories about Jesus were being read by Christians. For example, the *Gospel According to James* says that as a boy Jesus cursed a playmate who had irreverently bumped into him and that the child fell dead. Graciously Jesus yielded to the pleas of the boy's parents and brought him to life again. The church rejected that Gospel. Luke's Acts of the Apostles was recognized as authoritative, but what about the *Acts of Peter* and the *Acts of John*? The latter described how John, on a missionary tour spending a night in an inn, found his bed inhabited. At his request the bed bugs marched out of the bed, arranged themselves in the corner of the room, and did not return until he granted them permission the next morning. Epistles like those of Clement were loved, and the *Shepherd of Hermas* was highly regarded. On the other hand, several books such as Revelation and 2 Peter that are now in our New Testament were the subject of controversy for centuries.

It was the heretic Marcion who, in the middle of the second century, first drew up a list of books as authoritative. An anti-Semite, he taught that the Jews' God of the Old Testament was a deity of wrath, a different God from the New Testament God of mercy. The Old Testament God had created this evil material world. Bodies are evil. Christ could not have been born from a woman, for that is a material process. Marcion drew up a list of books Christians should read. Of the four Gospels he accepted only Luke, and that in an edited version; Matthew was much too Jewish. Some letters of Paul seemed to him to support his views, but Hebrews and other books were not recommended. Marcion rejected the Old Testament; most in the church rejected Marcion. His followers remained a separate church for more than a century. His drawing up a canon may have pushed the church in the direction of drawing up one of their own.

The earliest list of Christian works regarded as authoritative by the orthodox majority of Christians is the Muratorian Canon, dating from near the end of the second century. In general it is identical with our New Testament. It does not include, however, James, 3 John, or Hebrews. Another writing of Peter is said to be disputed, though it is not clear whether this refers to 2 Peter or a now lost *Apocalypse of Peter.* Dispute about whether to include Revelation continued for centuries. The Muratorian Canon also included one book from the Apocrypha, the Wisdom of Solomon. (The Apocrypha is a collection of books that come to us from Greek manuscripts, unlike the canonical Old Testament, which was written in Hebrew and Aramaic. Evidently many Greek-speaking Jews loved the apocryphal books, but these books did not continue to be regarded by the Jews as authoritative in a way comparable to that of the Hebrew Scriptures.)

The adoption of the canon came about more by usage than by ecclesiastical decree. The books that make up the canonical New Testament were quoted over and over by the preachers and writers of the church from the second century on. The oldest authoritative list of books that exactly agrees with the New Testament canon of today is that of Bishop Athanasius in 367. Only later did various synods and popes officially endorse it.

One highly important development was the translation of the Bible into Latin, which had replaced Greek as the language best known in the western part of the empire. About AD 386 an ascetic monk named Jerome took up residence in a cave in Bethlehem, where he founded a fellowship of monks. His wealthy patron and friend Paula joined him and formed her associates into a fellowship of sisters. Jerome reported that Paula could read Hebrew almost as well as he. (A delightful legend says that he bandaged the paw of a wounded lion and had a lion for a pet the rest of his life!) There had already been some translations into Latin, most of them from the Septuagint, the Greek version of the Old Testament. Jerome, however, determined to translate from the original Hebrew. His work was called the *Vulgate*, that is, the Bible for the common people, the vulgar. Though at first many people rejected it, throughout the church in western Europe for a thousand years Jerome's Vulgate became *the* Bible. He himself rejected the Apocrypha, but at the insistence of some bishops included some of it. Eventually others added the apocryphal books to their editions of the Vulgate. Thus they too became part of the canon, the rule of faith, for the "Catholic" (universal) church. (At the time of the Reformation Protestants were to reject that addition of the Apocrypha as authority.)

Chapter divisions were not inserted into the Scriptures until the thirteenth century, and verse divisions were added by a Paris printer in the sixteenth.

Setting Standards for the Church: The Creeds

The Pastoral Epistles quote what may be little creeds, encouraging their use in order to guard the faith. It is only legend that the the Apostles' Creed, beloved by the church for so many centuries, was composed by the apostles themselves. Shorter forms of that creed appear in the second century, and it apparently evolved as baptismal vows for candidates for church membership.

Though the church had bishops to teach sound doctrine, the bishops did not always agree. The church began to recognize authoritative Scriptures, but as early as the writing of 2 Peter 3:16 it was noted that in the epistles of Paul there were some things "hard to understand." Was Jesus a divine being, or was he human? The gnostics were too "spiritual" to believe that Jesus was as human as we. They said that Christ only appeared to die. The Great Commission of Matthew 28:19 commanded that the church baptize "in the name of the Father and of the Son and of the Holy Spirit." Were these three gods, or, if not, in what sense were they one and yet three? In the second half of the second century the theologian Tertullian first used the word "Trinity" of God. Was God, some wondered, first the Creator-Father, then became the Son, and is now the Holy Spirit?

One of the great threats to what became orthodox Christianity was Arianism. Early in the fourth century a priest named Arius proposed a solution to the problem of the Trinity: all three were divine, but the Father is supreme and eternal, existing before the Son, and the Holy Spirit is only third in rank. Concerning the Son he said, "There was when he was not"; the Father preceded all. Jesus Christ was not of the *same* "substance" (essential being) as God the

Father, though he was of *similar* "substance." In effect he was saying that Jesus was like God but not quite the same as God. Arianism spread over the empire. Popular choruses sang the Arian theology. Governmental leaders joined bishops in the controversy.

Constantine was distressed. He had hoped that the empire could be united through the Christian faith, and now the church itself was being split. To remedy that situation, in 325 he summoned bishops to Nicea to what came to be called "the First Ecumenical Council."

It must have been a colorful assembly. There, again, were the Roman police with their swords drawn, surrounding the Christians. But this time it was not for persecution; these soldiers were a guard of honor for the assembling bishops. According to tradition, 318 delegates came, one for every circumcised person in Abraham's household, plus one for the Holy Spirit. The bishops now rode like senators in chariots provided at government expense.

Saint Nicholas himself was there—to be known later as "Santa Claus." So was Paphnutius, blinded in one eye during the persecution under the emperor Diocletian. Emperor Constantine kissed his eyeless cheek. One bishop did not speak during the conference; Roman persecutors had cut out his tongue.

At Nicea the leader of the fight against Arianism was a bishop named Athanasius. His life was so dedicated to that battle that some nicknamed him "Athanasius-Against-the-World." One result of the Council of Nicea was the Nicene Creed, almost in its present form. It affirmed faith in the humanity of Jesus Christ, but stated clearly that he is "Very God of Very God; Begotten, not made; Being of one substance with the Father, by whom all things were made." Millions still recite the creed, but few include the original's closing curse: "And those that say, 'There was when he was not' . . . or . . . that the Son is 'of another substance . . .' these the Catholic church anathematizes [damns]."

Not everybody immediately agreed. Some bishops, supported by governors, resisted. One of Constantine's successors was an Arian, and for much of his brief reign Arianism seemed to be orthodoxy. Athanasius was pursued by the authorities. Once the police approached the boat in which he was making his escape. "Have you seen Athanasius?" they called. "Yes," one of the boatmen replied, "and he is not far from you." The police sped past hoping to catch up with the fugitive theologian.

In 381 the Council of Constantinople reaffirmed the "one substance" formula and added an affirmation that the same might be said of the Holy Spirit. By such standards the church secured the basic doctrines of the faith.

The church's creeds were worded in the abstract language of philosophy. They defined, however, a faith that changed lives. One convert wrote of his experience:

I was involved in such a mass of errors from my earlier life, and they were holding me. I did not even myself believe that I could win free. . . . Then came the water of regeneration, and the stain of my past life was washed away. A light from above, both bright and clear, shed itself on my heart, now reconciled. Then, by the Spirit breathed from heaven, a second birth made me anew, a different man, and, in a wonderful way. What in me had wavered now stood firm.[11]

By the end of the fourth century the church had survived persecution, converted even its persecutors, and built a wall of ecclesiastical government, Scripture, and creeds to define and preserve its faith. It needed them, because the empire that supported it was on the brink of disaster.

Questions Chapter 2

1. This chapter begins with a quotation from an anonymous Christian about the life he saw among believers in the second century. Of what passages of Scripture does it remind you?
2. What can you deduce about second-century Christians from the correspondence between Governor Pliny and Emperor Trajan? Why would some accept death rather than lie about their faith? (Remember prayerfully that Christians, including many thousands of Presbyterians, face persecution in many lands today.)
3. Which stories or people in this chapter are your favorites, and what can we learn from them? What can we learn from some that are not your favorites?
4. In what ways does it seem to you that the accession of a Constantine to the throne was good for the church, and in what ways does it seem to have been dangerous?
5. How did we get the Bible? According to Luke 1:1–4 how and when was his Gospel written? As implied by 2 Pet. 3:15–16, how soon were the letters of Paul being collected?
6. This chapter ends with the testimony of an early convert. How is it like your own experience, or that of some other Christian you know?

Chapter 3

Monks, Missionaries, and Other Saints (c. 400–1100)

*I*n AD 410 the Mediterranean world heard shocking news: Aleric and his Visigoths had sacked Rome. For centuries Rome had seemed "the eternal city." It had founded what seemed an invincible empire. Although nearly one hundred years earlier, Constantine had moved the capital east to a city he had built, Constantinople, even earlier the empire had begun to decline. Still to many in the west the report of the sacking of Rome must have been devastating. Christendom was moving into what some historians have called "the Dark Ages."

Paradoxically, the news stimulated the writing of the work that, outside the Bible itself, was to become perhaps the most influential book in all of Christian theology. Aleric had sacked the city of Rome, but now Augustine wrote of *The City of God*.

Augustine

There were people who had their own explanation of why Rome had fallen: it had abandoned its gods for the Christian God—a God who could not save it. Augustine, bishop of Hippo in North Africa, now set out to answer that charge. Rome had endured for centuries, he argued, by the mercy of God, an earthly reward because many Romans had indeed practiced lives of virtue. Now, however, God had brought upon it the judgment its pride and selfishness deserved. Far from causing its destruction, the Christian faith of many had saved them. Hundreds had sought sanctuary in churches, where the Visigoths had spared them.

Any human society built on pride and love of self, Augustine argued, is bound for destruction. It is the "city" of this world. There is also, however, another "city." Its citizens are the true church, those who live their lives in faith in God. The city of this world is temporal, but the city of God is eternal. Rome may fall, but the kingdom of God will stand forever. To it all peoples are summoned to give their allegiance. Though dispersed throughout the world, the city of God, the church, is a united, holy, and eternal nation.

Augustine did not intend quite to equate the visible church of which he was a bishop with the city of God. He was aware there were members of the church whose allegiance was really to this world. But in so far as the church was "the body of Christ," the kingdom of God was a reality right here on this sinful earth; it is the city of God.

Augustine recognized the wisdom of some philosophers, especially Plato. Nevertheless, for a knowledge of the true God, he maintained, we must turn to "the Scripture, which excels all the writings of all nations by its divine authority."[1] Its authority comes from Christ himself, the mediator. Augustine reviewed the whole Bible as the history of the two "cities." For Augustine the Bible tells a story of which we ourselves are now a part.

Even Satan was good by creation, though he became wicked by his own will. He fell, and tempted Adam also to choose sin. Yet even this was in accord with the plan of the all-wise God, who can use evil to achieve even greater good.

Humankind was created rational and blessed, with the gift of free will. "From the bad use of free will there originated the whole train of evil."[2] Though at times Augustine seems to make sex the original sin, he does carefully affirm that "it was not the corruptible flesh that made the soul sinful, but the sinful soul that made the flesh corruptible."[3] Pride is the beginning of sin. "By craving to be more, man becomes less; and by aspiring to be self-sufficing, he fell away from Him who truly suffices him."[4] With sin came death and all our woes. After Adam's fall we are free to make choices among evils, but we children of Adam can never really choose not to sin.

After lengthy discussion of original sin, this guilt and corruption common to all children of Adam, Augustine now reviews the whole of Scripture as the story of the two kingdoms, the whole history being in accord with the plan and foreknowledge of God. Repeatedly God's grace intervened in behalf of humankind. The story of Noah and the ark is a kind of picture of Christ and the church, saved by grace. Jerusalem failed to be the city of God. God raised up prophets to call Israel to righteousness, and they promised that a Savior would come. That Savior did come. The Holy Spirit now endowed those in Christ with new lives. That life was not a reward or a result of their choice but a gift of God's grace infused into the elect.

With Christ's coming Satan was bound. According to Augustine, the "thousand years" referred to in Revelation 20 is the period of the church today, the church militant, the kingdom of God on earth. We ourselves are now engaged in its battle, which takes place within human souls. At the end of the millennium Christ will come again, the dead will be raised, and there will be a judgment, some given eternal life and some eternal punishment. Everything has happened and will happen according to the gracious plan and will of the sovereign God. It is a continuing story.

Pelagius, a presbyter in Britain, argued for a quite different view. Augustine's doctrine of predestination, he felt, denied our moral responsibility. God's grace is more a matter of God's giving us guidance; we have free will to choose whether we will obey. There is no original sin come down upon us from Adam. Perfection, Pelagius argued, is possible, else God would not command it. God's grace rewards those who repeatedly choose to do God's will. Eventually the church condemned Pelagianism, but many advocated what came to be called "semi-Pelagianism." This view proposed that at least each person's initial decision to accept or reject salvation was made by that individual's free will.

Augustine saw any compromise as comparable to the salvation by works of the law against which Paul had fought. Faith itself is always a free, unchosen gift of God. Augustine's view was in part the result of his own experience. In his *Confessions* he wrote a spiritual autobiography addressed to God. "Thou hast formed us for Thyself, and our hearts are restless till they find rest in Thee."[5] That restlessness was akin to what Paul describes, "I do not do what I want, but I do the very thing I hate" (Rom. 7:15). He tells how in his childhood he and a group of boys stole all the pears off a neighbor's tree. It was not because they wanted to eat them all, for they destroyed most of them; their vandalism was because of their sinful nature. "It was foul, and I loved it."[6] He even confessed that he sinned in his dreams! One barrier to becoming a Christian was his reluctance to give up his mistress.

At length, however, the prayers of his mother, Monica, were answered. One day he was praying under a fig tree when he heard a child's voice chanting as if in a game, "Take up and read; take up and read." He opened his Bible to these words of Paul: "'Not in rioting and drunkenness, not in chambering and wantonness, not in strife and envying; but put ye on the Lord Jesus Christ, and make not provision for the flesh, to fulfill the lusts thereof.' No further would I read, nor did I need; for instantly, as the sentence ended—by a light, as it were, of security infused into my heart—all the gloom of doubt vanished away."[7] It was not by his choice but rather in spite of his sinful will that he had been won by Christ.

Officially Augustinianism finally won the battle. The church, however, eventually arrived at the view that with baptism God's grace freely washed away our sin that comes from Adam. Each of us, however, must pay, in this life or in purgatory, for the sins we commit. The church alone, of course, could administer saving baptism. It was not until Luther and Calvin that Augustine's emphasis on grace alone for salvation was so emphasized. Meanwhile saints spread the gospel as they understood it and baptized sinners throughout pagan Europe.

Monasteries

Readers of Acts know that Paul lived in a time when the Roman Empire imposed a high degree of law and order on the Mediterranean world. Paul could travel in relative safety from place to place, and Roman officials could protect him on occasion from mob violence. He could write letters, assured that in every congregation there would be at least some people who could read them aloud to the others. Greek was the language of empire-wide trade, so he could preach without an interpreter in every city he came to.

As Augustine had feared, with the fall of Rome that era of order, learning, and unity drew to a close. Some historians protest the use of the term "Dark Ages" to describe the Europe of the next few centuries. Nevertheless, the disintegration of the empire was a blow to the civilization Greek culture and Roman government had achieved. What kept the light of learning and of the orthodox Christianity of Nicea alive was, more than anything else, the development of monasteries in many places throughout Europe.

Earlier there had been the Anchorites, individual ascetics who had separated themselves from all temptations of the flesh and who devoted themselves to prayer. In the fourth century Pachomius gathered a group of his followers into a holy community. In the sixth century Benedict provided a model that was to guide thousands of monasteries and convents throughout the world and into the twenty-first century. He established a monastery on Mount Cassino in Italy, cutting down a grove sacred to pagans and overturning their altar. Soon he was joined by his sister, Scholastica, who established a similar community for women. Benedict drew up a set of rules that, with some variations, has been used by many monasteries on down to the present day.

If you had been a monk in a Benedictine monastery you would have risen for prayer at 2 o'clock each morning, though since you went to bed about 6:30 each night this did not mean much loss of sleep. You would spend the next three hours in meditation and in the community's prayers. From five to nine you would study. From 9:15 to noon you would work, often in the fields, whose products supported the monastery. You were provided one or perhaps two meals a day, with two cooked dishes and perhaps fresh fruits or vegetables. You would never speak during a meal; one of the community would read from some uplifting work. From time to time you would have to take your turn working for a week in the kitchen. After the noon meal you could have an hour's rest, and then you would go to work again. Compline, the prayer to close the day, preceded the 6:30 bedtime. You would have a knife with which to eat and work. It was strictly forbidden to hide it under your pillow in the common dormitory in which you slept; with armed men together one might get hurt. If you were a woman in a convent your life would be much like that of men in a monastery.

Benedict thought of holiness not so much in terms of overcoming the lusts of the flesh as in service. Your service might be not in the fields but teaching the boys of the neighborhood. If you were a priest you might minister as pastor. You might spend your life copying manuscripts, especially the Gospels and other books of the Bible. The reverence in which the monks held Scripture is witnessed to by the ornate, beautifully illustrated copies that they preserved for us. Monks loved the Psalms, and their worship so centered on them that you would probably come to know the Psalter by heart. Though you were forbidden to travel, your monastery often provided hospitality for others. You might be engaged in ministry to the poor, and you might be involved in caring for the sick. You individually would own nothing, not even the underwear you wore; all things were the common property of the monastery.

You would be ruled over by an abbot. His word was absolute, but Benedictine tradition had instructed him to be kind, and in what seemed to him especially important matters he would confer with you and the other monks. Once you were in, you were there for life; only by permission of the abbot were you permitted to leave, even for another monastery. (The monasteries' stability helped give one bit of stability to an often chaotic Europe.) If you were guilty of breaking a rule the kindly abbot was supposed to see that you were admonished privately. If you disobeyed a third time you were to be reprimanded before the whole community. If you continued long enough unrepentant you might be whipped, but only as a last resort would you be ejected from the monastery.

Monks cleared forests and planted crops, and monasteries aimed at being self-supporting. Many people, however, gave them gifts, including large tracts of land, often tended by serfs. Eventually some monasteries became so wealthy that there was a temptation to the very worldliness monks had entered to escape.

Missionaries

Monasteries often provided the missionaries that undertook, with considerable success, to win pagans and heretics to the orthodox Christianity of the Nicene Creed. (The Arian heretical form of Christianity also spread among barbarians.) The church has always loved stories of these missionaries, heroes of the faith.

Patrick has left us his own account of how in the fifth century he brought the gospel to Ireland. He was born in Scotland or near the border in England, the son of a deacon and the grandson of an elder, but, he confesses, "I did not know the true God." Pirates kidnaped him when he was a youth of sixteen, and for six years he tended sheep as a slave in Ireland. "By day I prayed a hundred prayers and as many at night."[8] Encouraged by a dream, he escaped, traveled two hundred miles to a port, was employed as a sailor, and at last reached home. One night he had another dream. Voices of Ireland were crying to him, "We beseech thee, holy youth, to come and walk with us once more."[9] Trained now and ordained as a priest, he returned to the land where once he had been a slave. There are many fanciful legends of his work in Ireland, including that he rid the island of its snakes. It is historical fact that he and others were very successful there. Ireland became a Christian center of learning when much of Europe was in ignorance and disorder. Patrick is buried in a Church of England (Episcopal) churchyard in north Ireland.

From Ireland missionaries spread the gospel. Columba established a monastery on the island of Iona. From there he and his fellow missionaries began to win that most backward of the barbarians, the people of Scotland. Legend says that in 563, on the last day of his life, a life full of hardships and danger, the old man was still copying Scripture, this time the Psalms. He had reached Psalm 34:10: "Those who seek the Lord lack no good thing." "There I must stop," he said. A bit later his brother monks found that he had died, but with a smile of joy on his face.

About the time Patrick was at work in Ireland, Queen Clothilde in what is now France was pleading with her husband Clovis to become a Christian. According to an ancient report, in a battle with some south German tribesmen his army was about to be wiped out. Desperate, he prayed to the Christ to whom his wife was devoted, promising to become a Christian if Christ would give him the victory. Victorious, he returned to tell his wife the story. Clothilde quickly summoned Remigius, bishop of Rheims, who instructed King Clovis in the orthodox, Nicene faith. When the king was baptized most of his subjects followed suit.

Another woman, Queen Theodolinda, won her husband, King Agiluf, and with his conversion his subjects, the Lombards, soon became Christians.

As in France, so in England a woman was instrumental in the conversion of a nation. About AD 600 Pope Gregory I sent a monk named Augustine—usually called Augustine of Canterbury to distinguish him from the earlier Augustine of Hippo—to be a missionary to England. The journey was so difficult and dangerous that Augustine turned around and went back, begging to be spared. Gregory, however, was determined, and at length Augustine gained an audience with King Ethelbert of Kent. Queen Bertha had already been attempting to win him to Christ. It is not certain whether Ethelbert actually became a Christian, but at least he granted the eloquent missionary freedom to spread the gospel. The daughter of Bertha and Ethelbert converted her husband, the king of Northumbria. Ethelbert's stronghold, Canterbury, continues to be the seat of the archbishop of the Church of England, mother of the Episcopal Church in America.

The great missionary to Germany was an Anglo-Saxon priest named Willibard. The pope gave him the name Boniface (doer of good deeds), and in 722 commissioned him to his task. The ancient legend says that Boniface cut down the oak of Thor, regarded as sacred by the pagans. From its timber he built a chapel for the true God. What is certain is that he was martyred at last. As Norman Langford retells the story, Boniface spoke to the men who would die with him that day: "Be strong in the Lord, and suffer willingly that which he permits . . . Brothers, be of a brave mind, and fear not those that kill the body, but cannot kill the soul that has an endless life. Rejoice in the Lord, and fix on him the anchor of your hope."[10]

Sometimes converts were made by the sword. On Christmas Day, AD 800, the pope crowned Charlemagne (Charles the Great of France) with the title "Emperor of the Romans." For more than three centuries there had been no real emperor in Rome. Now, with the patronage of the church, Charlemagne undertook to rebuild the Roman Empire. He was remarkably successful, though his "Holy Roman Empire" was not very holy and was not really Roman. He was determined to be a Christian emperor, and as such he supported the church in every way. He decreed that there should be preaching in the language of the people, made Sunday a day of rest, and collected tithes like taxes. He built and reformed schools, decreeing that there should be a school for every church, open to rich and poor alike. Charlemagne also regarded himself as called to spread the gospel. This he did to his own satisfaction by a series of bloody conquests, forcing those whom he defeated to be baptized or die.

In many places people became church members not so much from personal decision to follow Christ as by conformity to the will of their rulers. Thus through sacrificial missionaries but also through conquest and royal decrees Europe became Christendom.

The Authority of the Pope

One result of the growth of the church in the West was growth of the power of the pope. For centuries the bishop of Rome had been claiming that authority. Eusebius tells us that about the year 175 Hegesippus wrote that the bishops are successors of the apostles. About 341 Julius, bishop of Rome, wrote to the council of Antioch that they had not acted in accordance with the tradition handed down from Peter, a tradition that he claimed to represent. Some sixty years later Jerome addressed the pope with awe and reverence because he was successor of Peter, "the rock on which the church was founded." Though at first the title "Pope" might be used of any bishop, it came to be exclusively the title of the bishop of Rome. The apostles had been succeeded by bishops, and the bishop of Rome, regarded as the heir of Peter, the chief of the apostles, eventually began to claim that he was the head of the whole church.

The pope not only claimed authority but was more and more able to exercise it. Monasteries and monastic orders were often directly related not simply to the local bishop but to the pope. Many of the missionaries who won western Europe were sent out under the auspices of the pope. Roman Catholicism was not the only kind of Christianity. Ireland and Scotland had never been part of the Roman Empire, and Christianity there had taken a somewhat different form. In Ireland there were monastic communities that included women as well as men, married and unmarried. They celebrated Easter on a different day. Their Celtic Christianity sometimes tended toward a more Pelagian theology. At the Council of Whitby in 663 representatives of the two types made their case before King Oswy of Northumbria. The Celtic Christians argued their case on the authority of Columba, who had brought the faith to Scotland. The representative of Rome, however, countered that the bishop of Rome was the successor of Peter, acknowledged head of the original apostles. Columba, the Scots admitted, could make no such claim. That won the debate: the British isles would be Roman Catholic.

One other factor in the spread of the idea of the supremacy of the pope was an eighth-century document called the *Donation of Constantine.* All scholars today acknowledge that it was a forgery, but for centuries it was accepted as authentic. It claimed that Emperor Constantine had contracted leprosy, but he had been instantly cured by baptism by Pope Sylvester. Grateful, when he moved his capital to Constantinople he announced that he would donate to the pope his palace, and all provinces, palaces, and districts of the city of Rome and Italy and of the regions of the West, and this authority should continue to his successors. Constantine would rule in the East, the pope in the West. For centuries few questioned that this spurious document recorded fact.

Church and State

The alliance between emperor and pope was based in part on mutual self-interest. In exchange for coronation, in the eighth century Pepin III granted civil government of a large area in Italy to the pope. The pope crowned Charlemagne,

Pepin's son, giving him the title "Emperor." Soon, however, their interests began to conflict. Each claimed full authority over the other. Charlemagne appointed bishops, and at first the pope agreed in his right to do this. Eventually the emperor claimed the right to appoint popes. The pope claimed that rulers could hold office only so long as they were in agreement with the pope.

The conflict came to a dramatic climax with Emperor Henry IV standing barefooted in the snow outside the papal palace. Determined to reform the church, Pope Gregory VII had decreed that priests must no longer be married, that the clergy must no longer buy offices, and that the pope, not the emperor, should appoint bishops. The German clergy rebelled at the decree against their marriage. Emperor Henry appointed a bishop in Milan. He announced that Gregory was no longer pope but a false monk. The pope excommunicated Henry, freeing Henry's subjects from any duty to obey that emperor. To secure his hold on his empire, in December 1077 Henry stood four days as a penitent, barefoot in the snow outside the pope's castle in Conossa, until the pope forgave him and withdrew the decree. When rebellion broke out back in Germany, the pope supported the rebels. Henry won the day, was excommunicated again by the pope, and this time invaded Rome and forced Pope Gregory to flee. A rival pope, Clement III, was elected to office, and Gregory died in exile. Conflict of church and state would continue down into the present.

Christianity in the East

One vast area never accepted the supremacy of the bishop of Rome. A century before Alaric sacked Rome, Constantine had moved the capital to a city of his own choosing, Byzantium, or, as he called it, Constantinople (today Istanbul). The people of the East called themselves Romans, and they would not have thought of the Roman Empire as falling because of the repeated sacking of faraway Rome. In the East the empire continued. Some of its churches were older than that of Rome itself.

In Greece and other parts of that Eastern empire a Christianity somewhat different from Roman Catholicism flourished. Not Latin but Greek, the language of the earliest churches, was the language of the people and of the liturgy. The bishop of Constantinople claimed to be its spiritual head, but the emperor in Constantinople actually controlled the church. The Eastern churches came to be called Orthodox as over against Roman Catholic. Nestorians, regarded as in error in their view of the nature of Christ, and other heretics spread their doctrines in the East.

After Constantine's death the empire in the East waned, and churches of different ethnic groups and languages developed. In the sixth century Constantinople's power revived. Theodora, a former actress—perhaps she had even been a courtesan—became queen and eagerly joined her husband Justinian to build up the grandeur of the church at Constantinople. The original church of Saint Sophia had burned. Theodora and Justinian resolved to build it in a far more glorious manner. Within forty days after the fire they began, employing a thousand workers. The Church of Saint Sophia was built not in the long, narrow basilica form of Western churches but under a round dome with smaller domes around it. Brilliant mosaics shone from its walls. Though now a museum, it still stands as a tribute to the magnificence of Byzantine Christianity. Tradition says that the pagan Vladimir I of Russia investigated Orthodox Christianity. He sent a delegation to Constantinople, and they returned with so glowing a report of the glories of Saint Sophia that in 988 he was baptized into Orthodoxy. A whole type of art and architecture became known as Byzantine.

The seventh century brought a blow to the church in the East from which it has never fully recovered. The church had spread into Persia, and some intrepid missionaries had even preached in China. In the year 613, however, an Arab named Muhammad began having mystical experiences; an angel, he said, was dictating to him the beautiful poetry that became the Koran. The Christian church he saw around him was decadent, worshiping images and often led by ignorant priests. He denounced its idolatry. The worship of the Trinity seemed to him to be polytheism. Jesus, he announced, was indeed a prophet, but it was blasphemy to speak of Allah as having a son. Followers rallied to his preaching, and Muslim missionaries set out to convert the world. Inevitably military conquests followed, with Islam accompanying the conquerors. Islam replaced much of the church in the East. Muslim armies swept over North Africa. At one time they reached as far as Vienna in central Europe, and they penetrated far into Spain in the west. In 732 the invasion in Spain was repelled, but the Eastern churches never recovered. Much of Asia remains predominantly, even exclusively, Muslim. In Palestine, Lebanon, Egypt, Turkey, and even Iraq smaller but heroic churches have held on, always as minorities and sometimes in spite of persecution. (Four Iraqi churches are counted as Presbyterian.)

Inevitably the division of the Roman Empire resulted in the division of the church. The final dispute centered around the fact that the West added to the Nicene Creed a clause stating that the Spirit proceeds not only from the Father but also from the Son. The bishop (patriarch) of Constantinople resisted. In 1054 the bishop of Rome excommunicated the bishop of

Constantinople, consigning him and his heretics to damnation with the devil. The bishop of Constantinople excommunicated and damned the pope. Though progress has been made, the rift between Roman Catholicism and Eastern Orthodoxy has never fully healed.

The Life of Christians

Popes feuded with kings and bishops feuded with one another, but day after day ordinary Christians worshiped God. There was indeed corruption in the church, but Christianity spread and was nourished throughout Europe. Typically church buildings were the center of the village, and the church was to a large extent the center of many people's lives. Every Sunday almost everyone attended mass. There they saw dramatized the sacrificial death of their Lord and his resurrection. There they fed upon his body. The mystic ceremonies carried out by the priests were in Latin, but the beauty of the Latin mass lifted hearts to God. The sermons were in the language of the people, and in them they heard the gospel and the call to righteous living. There were, of course, unworthy monks and priests, but there were hundreds of thousands whose lives bore witness to the gospel. Until about AD 1000, many priests were married, presenting sometimes a model of family life.

Most people could not read. The question of the use of images was debated. The East decided that statues were too nearly idols, but in those Orthodox churches there were many icons (pictures). These often screened much of the priests' mysterious ceremonies from the common laity, but they pictured Christ, the Virgin, and the saints for the people's guidance and worship. In the West statues were permitted. Images are the books of the unlearned, they argued, sermons in wood and stone that proclaim the gospel.

There were compromises of a sort. As late as AD 600 there were pagans who marked their new year on November 1 with a festival to the dead. The night before there would be parties, with masks and bobbing for apples and gifts of food for visitors from the underworld. The church decided to make November 1 the day of the Feast of All Saints. The night before, All Hallows (Saints) Eve, continued as Halloween, and All Saints Day commemorated heroes of the faith.

Monasteries not only preserved learning in their own ranks but often offered schools to the boys of the neighborhood. Their sister convents offered the one career outside the home available to most women. During the week many women worshiped in the mass the priest offered daily, and there they found fellowship not only with God but with one another. Women were excluded from the clergy, but the worship of the Virgin Mary gave women a sense of one like themselves who had special access to the Lord. Christ might be the Judge of the world, but Mary, they believed, was always compassionate and could win for her devotees her Son's mercy.

In the Middle Ages Christ was often pictured as a stern judge. The veneration of the saints gave many a sense of something closer to them through which they might have access to the exalted Lord. Used to many gods for many purposes, pagan converts enjoyed the thought of saints who had in some sense experienced their own problems and held firm in spite of them. A modern list of saints whom Roman Catholics relate to special needs include such heroes and heroines of the past as these: for craftsmen, St. Roch; for grave diggers, Anthony the Abbot; for leather workers, St. Crispin; for sufferers from rheumatism, St. James the Greater; for those with toothaches, St. Apollonia; and for victims of nervous disorders, St.Vitus.

If you had worshiped in a medieval church the sermon might warn you against the seven deadly sins: pride, greed, luxury, envy, gluttony, anger, and despair. The priest would exhort you to practice the seven cardinal virtues: four from the Greek philosophers—wisdom, courage, self-control, and justice; and three from the New Testament—faith, hope, and love. You would be taught to practice the seven works of mercy: feed the hungry, give drink to the thirsty, clothe the naked, visit the sick, house the homeless, ransom captives, and bury the dead. If you realized that your life did not measure up to the standards of the faith, and if you truly repented and confessed your sins to God's representative, the priest, the priest would pray for you, assure you of Christ's merciful pardon, and assign you some good deed to compensate for your faults. Even at death the priest would be there, hearing your final confession, anointing you with holy oil, and assuring you of life eternal.

In an age when this life was short and hard the hope of heaven was very much a part of the faith. The Venerable Bede records a story of the meeting of the missionary Paulinus with Edwin, king of Northumbria, and his advisors. One of his counselors, Bede reports, gave this advice:

> The present life of man, O king, seems to me, in comparison of that time which is unknown to us, like to the swift flight of a sparrow through the room wherein you sit at supper in winter, with your commanders and ministers, and a good fire in the midst, whilst the storms of rain and snow prevail abroad; the sparrow, I say, flying in at one door, and immediately out at another, whilst he is within, is safe from the wintry storm; but after a short space of fair weather, he immediately vanished out of your sight, into the dark winter from which he had emerged. So this life of man appears for a short space, but of what went before, or of what is to follow we are utterly

ignorant. If, therefore, this new doctrine contains something more certain, it seems justly to deserve to be followed.[11]

Since he was writing about a century after the event, we cannot be sure that the Venerable Bede was quoting accurately. We can safely assume that his story of the promise of eternal life reflects something of the faith that won medieval Europe.

Perhaps the best piety of the time is reflected in the prayer in which nuns expressed their ideal: "Almighty God, Father, Son, and Holy Spirit, who are power, wisdom, and love, inspire in me these three things; power to serve thee, wisdom to please thee, and love to do it; power that I may do, wisdom that I may know what to do, and love that I may be moved to do all that is pleasing to thee."[12]

There was light in "the Dark Ages"!

Questions Chapter 3

1. In what sense, if any, does it seem to you that the church is "the city of God," in sharp contrast to any "city of this world," including America?
2. How do Presbyterian confessions echo major ideas of Augustine, including his controversial ideas that God rules in history and that even our choice to believe is entirely a gift of God's grace?
3. Taizé in France is a kind of monastery somewhat like those of the Middle Ages, sponsored in part by Presbyterians. How would you react to a proposal that we establish one in America?
4. Here are some arguments that have been used against world missions: "What right have we to say our religion is better than theirs?" "We have plenty to do here in our country first." "Missions cost too much in lives and money." Why did these not stop those who brought the gospel to our ancestors? How valid are they for international mission work now?
5. In the 2004 presidential campaign a Catholic bishop forbad his priests to serve Communion to a Catholic candidate because he disagreed with certain stands of the church. Church-state cases come every year before the Supreme Court. What light does this chapter shed on church-state relations?
6. What stories, people, or ideas in this chapter did you find most interesting?

Chapter 4

Crusades, Colleges, and Cathedrals (c. 1100–1500)

*I*n 1095 Pope Urban II proclaimed a great new project in which all Christians should engage. The church, he knew, needed rebuilding. Much of the East had been overrun by a people who, he charged, were monstrous pagans, abusing and even slaughtering the people of God. The holy sepulcher of our Lord had fallen into their evil hands. All Christian Europe must rally for a great crusade to deliver the oppressed and rescue the world's most holy places. All who might die in this holy war, fighting for God, he promised, would have their sins forgiven and go immediately to heaven.

The battle cry went up throughout much of the church, "God wills it!"

The Crusades

For many years the church had tried to limit wars, yet European nobles had for centuries been killing each other. Augustine's "just war" theory had not deterred them; each could claim that his cause was just. A treaty called "The Truce of God" urged that there be no fighting on weekends, holy days, or Lent. Another, "The Peace of God," tried to protect women, priests, monks, old people, farmers, livestock, and agricultural equipment. When King Richard the Lion-Hearted was killed, some said that his death was God's judgment on him because he had been fighting during Lent. The church attempted to enforce its limits on fighting. It even developed a kind of priestly police force, but to many warring lords the armed clerics seemed simply one more army. In one battle seven hundred priests were slain. "The Truce of God" and "The Peace of God" had failed. Now, however, a way had been found to unite Europe. All would join as brothers to slaughter not one another but the Muslims.

The First Crusade was successful. In 1099, just four years after the pope had called for the crusade, the Christians' army arrived at Jerusalem. First they laid siege to the city, hoping to starve its people into submission. After a month, however, they heard that a large Arab army was coming against them. Barefoot, they marched around the city singing penitential hymns. Having thus ensured, as they thought, God's help, they attacked. An eyewitness gives us this account of what followed:

> Some of our men (and this was more merciful) cut off the heads of their ene-
> mies; others shot them with arrows, so that they fell from the towers; oth-
> ers tortured them longer by casting them into the flames. Piles of heads,
> hands, and feet were to be seen in the streets of the city. . . . In the temple
> and portico of Solomon, men rode in blood up to their knees and the bridle
> reins. Indeed, it was a just and splendid judgment of God, that this place
> should be filled with the blood of unbelievers. . . . How [the victorious
> Christians] rejoiced and exulted and sang. . . . This day . . . marks the justi-
> fication of all Christianity.[1]

They found that many Jerusalem Jews had gathered together, praying; crusaders slaughtered them. One eyewitness boasts of the chastity of these holy
warriors that they did not vent their lusts on the young women; they simply
ran them through with their spears. Another makes a similar boast, saying that
the crusaders abstained from sexual intercourse except, he says, "as much as
health demanded." Others report, however, that rape did often occur.

Their Christian Kingdom of Jerusalem endured for nearly a century. It is
said that Christians had fared much better under Muslim rule than Muslims
did when the Christians were in control. In 1144, however, Edessa fell into
Muslim hands, so for a second crusade the church mustered two hundred
thousand holy warriors to win it back. They failed, and most were killed in
the attempt. Crusaders did succeed in slaughtering many Jews along the way.

In 1187 Saladin, a Saracen, took Jerusalem back into Muslim hands. There
followed a series of crusades, none of which was successful. The most pitiful
were the children's crusades. Stephen, a boy in France, announced that Christ
had appeared to him and assured him that children, by their innocence, could
win what swords and spears had not. God would work miracles for them. Thousands flocked to him, and another boy, named Nicholas, rallied others in Germany. Mostly twelve-year-olds, including some girls, they set out. Many lost
their lives to bandits and the other hardships of attempting to cross the Alps
into Italy. Thousands did reach Italy, though the German children turned back
at the command of the pope. Five thousand set sail for the Holy Land. Some
boats sank. The rest were diverted by cruel crews, who sold the children as
slaves; none reached Jerusalem. Eighteen years later one of the few survivors
could boast that not a single child had been willing to lighten his slavery by

renouncing the Christian faith for Islam. Their crusade had failed, but they had remained faithful. The last crusade did briefly regain control of Jerusalem, but its Christian king was eventually captured, forced to pay ransom, and in 1270 died of fever. There were no more major crusades against Palestine, but from time to time a pope would call for crusades against heretics.

New Learning

One positive result of western Europe's encounter with Islamic culture was considerable intellectual growth in Christendom. The centuries from the sixth through the twelfth are sometimes referred to as "the Dark Ages." Many priests were illiterate. One test for literary was to read a verse from the Psalms. One memorized the verse but was caught because when he pretended to read it he held the Bible upside down. Muslim lands, however, were intellectually far more advanced. One enduring gift of their scholars is the use of Arabic numerals, supplanting the West's awkward Roman ones.

Augustine had readily acknowledged his debt to Plato and the Platonists. Their kind of thought seemed suitable for thinking about the gospel. Plato had spoken of the "beatific vision," and that idea harmonized with the mysticism characteristic of many monks and nuns. The Muslims, however, had preserved the work of Aristotle, and study of his writings and his Muslim followers now began to make changes in European thinking. Great universities were developing, and with Latin the universal language of scholarship students and professors from many lands could understand and be understood in all the great centers of learning. Some advanced scholars qualified to be called "masters," and some "doctors." Traditionally historians classify the twelfth century as still part of what have been called "the Dark Ages." The thirteenth century, by contrast, was one of considerable enlightenment. With its monastic reforms, saints like Francis, the building of great cathedrals, the universal sway of the church over so much of ordinary life, and the new emphasis on education, some have called it the most Christian century in history.

One great university was in Paris. There, in the thirteenth century, Thomas Aquinas set out to explain and defend Roman Catholic theology by the use of Aristotelian logic. As a boy he had been called "a dumb ox." He was to become recognized, however, as probably the most original, thorough, and influential thinker since Augustine. Thomas was a Dominican. The Dominicans and the Franciscans were a new kind of order, not confined to monasteries but going out into the world seeking to teach, help the poor, and do good deeds. Thomas set himself the task of relating the "new" philosophy of Aristotle with the doctrines of Roman Catholicism. In a sense he was reconciling faith and the "science" of his day. He was remarkably successful. Point after point, he examined and undertook to disprove each counterargument; then with each he defended the orthodox Catholic position. His five "proofs" of the existence of God have been a basis of much of Christian apologetics ever since. Among these "proofs" was the argument that the existence of the world shows the work of a wise creator. Students came from all over the world to hear him lecture. Christianity, he was sure, is never unreasonable; indeed most of its doctrines could be proved rationally. He did readily agree, however, that at certain points revelation went *beyond* Aristotelian logic, but he argued that it was never *contrary to* reason. Students returned to spread his ideas around Europe. Though some scholars opposed his ideas, a detailed, systematic program of doctrine, supported by his philosophy, won approval from Rome and was to become known as scholasticism, the dogmatics of the schools.

Worship in 1300

Scholars learned, but all the people worshiped. If you had worshiped in the thirteenth or fourteenth century you might have attended mass in an elaborate and beautiful church. Your grandfather might have told you how as a little boy he had helped build it, pulling a wagon loaded with small stones. He had seen rich merchants and proud nobles sweating side by side with peasants as together they pulled huge stones into place. Your grandmother would have helped too. You would have loved the church, in part because it was a gift of your own family and your community to God. In most villages the church was at the center not simply in location but in the life of the community.

You might have worshiped in one of the great cathedrals that, so many centuries later, still inspire our awe and reverence. Seeing it from a distance the cathedral might have reminded you of a ship, the Noah's ark of faith bringing safety in the storms of the world. Every line of the cathedral would point you toward heaven. Great buttresses supported the high, pointed roof. As you entered your gaze would be drawn first to the altar; it contained, you believed, the very body of Christ. (A doctrine had developed, called "transubstantiation," that declared that the bread and wine were actually changed into Christ's body and blood.) Then your eyes would have been drawn upward, higher and higher by the pointed Gothic arches that lifted your thoughts toward God. All around, you would see statues of the twelve apostles and of other saints. The most prominent would be the image of the Blessed Virgin, the object of your devotion. Behind the altar you would see the cross, probably with the image of your Savior, twisted in agony, still suffering because of your sins. Before the Virgin and before some of the saints candles would be burning. You might light one as a prayer for the soul of your long departed grandfather. You might take your place in one of the transepts, the side sections of the church, for the building would be shaped like a cross. As the sun shone through stained-glass windows it would have seemed that the light of heaven itself was pouring down upon you. The windows' multicolored pictures were one way you had learned the stories of the Bible and of the saints. All your senses would be caught up in the worship. You would smell the incense, and the music of plainsongs sung by a great choir would greet you. Teams of richly robed priests would chant the mysteries of the Latin mass. At what would be for you the climactic moment, you would go forward and kneel before the altar, on which the body of your Lord had been offered afresh. Only the priests might drink of Christ's blood, lest it be spilled on the floor, but you would taste once again a bit of God's body in your mouth.

Some Ups and Downs of Papal Power

You might return from such worship to a poor home, but for centuries many bishops and the pope, "the Servant of the servants of God," had often lived in luxury. At times the papacy was dominated by a few nobles in Rome. In the tenth century, during an era sometimes called "the pornographic period," a prostitute named Marozia had such influence over those nobles that she was able to choose who the next pope would be. Charlemagne's father Pepin had granted secular rule of part of Italy to the pope. The pope defended his territory with an army frequently engaged in wars with surrounding city-states. Some popes led their troops into battle, and much of their wealth was spent on papal wars.

The papacy became rich. Bishoprics and other offices were often bought, a practice called simony. A bishop was expected to give half his first year's salary to the pope, and the pope could move him from place to place, collecting half a year's salary with each new appointment. Sometimes a position might be left vacant, because then the income that would have gone to the bishop would go to the pope. Nepotism, the appointment of family members to high-paying positions, became all too common. There were, however, popes and other leaders who were unselfish and dedicated Christians and sought to remove these abuses and reform the church.

The conflict between church and state continued. Kings claimed the right to appoint bishops; popes claimed the right to excommunicate kings. As the lands worked by serfs were the property of their lords, and those lords held their territories by authority of their kings, so the pope claimed that kings held their nations by authority of the pope. Many popes sought to keep church affairs under church control, not that of kings. In 1302, in his conflict with Philip of France, Pope Boniface issued the decree *Unam Sanctam.* There is but one church, he declared, with one Lord, Jesus Christ. Peter became the "vicar" (the one who takes the place) of Christ, and the popes are the successors of Peter. Allegorizing the passage in Luke 32:35–38, he announced that

> in this Church . . . are two swords, the spiritual and the temporal. . . . Both are in the power of the Church. . . . But the latter is to be used for the Church, the former by her; the former by the priest, the latter by kings and captains but at the will and by the permission of the priest. The one sword, then, should be under the other, and temporal authority subject to spiritual.[2]

King Philip burned the papal bull (decree). Pope Boniface prepared to excommunicate King Philip. The day before the excommunication was to be published, agents of the king kidnaped the pope and paraded him, seated backward on a horse, through the town. A mob sacked his home and that of some of his relatives. He was rescued and returned to Rome, but old and humiliated, he died soon thereafter. In 1309 there followed what came to be known as "the Babylonian Captivity of the Church." Dominated by the French king, popes lived not in Rome but in Avignon in France, where they built for themselves a luxurious palace. Not until 1377 did the pope return to Rome. Meanwhile the pope supported France in its war with England, and other nations chose up sides and entered the fight.

Urban VI succeeded to the papacy in 1378. Many cardinals did not like the reforms he proposed, so they elected a new pope. There were now two popes, one back in the palace in Avignon and one in Rome. Various nations and groups supported one or the other, and the popes were involved in armed conflict with each other. In an effort to stop this scandal, an attempt was made to depose both and set a new one on the throne in Rome. The result was that for a few years there were three popes! Finally, in 1414 the Council of Constance, supported by Emperor Sigismund, ended the schism, establishing one pope, living in Rome.

Monks and Mystics

Though the spectacle of warring popes was not edifying, the church provided the ordinary believer with many examples of complete self-sacrifice. Crusaders, however misguided, were men who were willing to leave home and family and give their lives in the service of Christ and his church. The monks, nuns, and their lay brothers and sisters in the monasteries and convents scattered through Europe displayed faith in a different way. Bernard of Clairvaux provides one example of twelfth-century devotion. Young Bernard gathered thirty friends, and they entered the monastery in Citeaux, France. In protest to the laxity of many monasteries, these monks, called Cistercians, determined to follow strictly the ancient rules of St. Benedict, and indeed to go beyond them in austerity and self-sacrifice. By example and by preaching and writing Bernard drew others. He himself founded 163 monasteries, and by the time of his death the number had grown to 343. Kings, bishops, and even popes looked to him for guidance. He traveled everywhere, preaching eloquently. He was among those whose zeal led to the Second Crusade. A mystic, he has left us writings that still inspire. Many earlier mystics had been caught up in a sense of unity with the One, the Almighty of heaven, or with the Virgin Mary. Bernard turned to the human Jesus. In contemplation of Jesus' life of meekness and self-denial and of his sacrificial death, Bernard believed, we ourselves may grow to become more like Christ. Millions of Christians still sing hymns attributed to Bernard: "O Sacred Head Now Wounded," "Jesus, Thou Joy of Loving Hearts," and "Jesus, the Very Thought of Thee."

Of the writings of the mystics of the late Middle Ages, one still read by millions is *The Imitation of Christ.* It is usually attributed to the fifteenth-century author Thomas à Kempis, though it may be based in part on earlier works. It begins:

> *He that followeth Me, walketh not in darkness,* saith the Lord. These are the words of Christ, by which we are admonished, how we ought to imitate His life and manners, if we would truly be enlightened, and delivered from all blindness of heart. Let therefore our chiefest endeavour be, to meditate upon the life of Jesus Christ. The doctrine of Christ exceedeth all the doctrine of holy men; and he that hath the Spirit will find therein *the hidden manna.*[3]

The church offered almost the only career available to women outside the home. The fourteenth-century saint Catherine of Siena worked among the poor and sick. She was personally charming, and soon she was guiding bishops and even popes. She pleaded with Pope Gregory XI to return from Avignon to Rome, and lived to see that dream of hers accomplished. She was so involved in affairs of church and state that at one time enemies attempted to assassinate her. She worked to end the strife among the rulers of Europe, at one point urging them to unite by joining in the Second Crusade.

Julian (Julia) of Norwich lived alone, an ascetic life, but her wisdom was sought by people of every rank. In her *Revelation of Love* she wrote:

> In this same time our Lord shewed to me a ghostly sight of his homely love-ing. I saw that he is to us everything that is good and comfortable for us. He is our clotheine that for love wrappith us, (halseth) us and all beclosyth us for tender love, that hee may never leave us, being to us althing that is gode, as to myne understondyng. Also in this he shewed a littil thing, the quanti-tye of an hesil nutt in the palme of my hand; and it was round as a balle. I lokid therupon with eye of my understondyng and thowte: "What may this be?" And it was generally answered thus: "It is all that is made." I marvel-lid how it might lesten, for methowte it might suddenly have fallen to nowte for littil. And I answered in my understondying: "It lesteth and ever shall, for God loveth it: and so allthing hath the being by the love of God." . . . The understondyng that I have in this sheweing: "God, of thy goodnesse, give me thyselfe; for thou art enow to me and I may nothing aske that is less that may be full worshippe to thee." . . . He . . . kepith us in his blissid love. And all this is of his goodness.[4]

Of all the saints of the Middle Ages, the one most loved still is Francis of Assisi. The son of a rich Italian merchant, as a youth he lived a life of luxury and worldly pleasure. Sobered by service in the war, he began more and more to devote himself—and his father's money—to helping the poor, even lepers. On a pilgrimage to Rome he had a dream in which he was called to build the church. He stole and sold a bale of his father's cloth and used the money for the rebuilding of a nearby church. Disgusted, his father took him to the bishop's court and denounced him. In response Francis renounced his inher-itance, even stripping off the clothes he was wearing. He would take "lady poverty" as his bride. Clad in the coarsest of robes, with a rope for a belt, and barefooted, he set out to minister to people in need. He himself would accept no money, only the food he needed for a day and clothes when his old ones wore out. One legend tells of a leper begging beside the road. Having noth-ing left to give, Francis passed him by. Suddenly Francis turned, got down on his knees beside the leper, and hugged him. "I love you," he said; love he could still give. Soon others joined him, and they set up headquarters near a leper colony. Francis ruled that they all must follow quite literally Jesus' direc-tions for traveling evangelists found in Matthew 10, and so they went from place to place barefoot and penniless, preaching repentance and the kingdom of God. Eventually the pope accepted these "minor brothers" as a new kind of order, which came to be called "friars." Clare, Francis's friend from Assisi, soon brought a group of young women to form a sister order, later known as the "Poor Clares."

Francis's goal was to become like Jesus, and in many ways he seems to have succeeded remarkably well. He sang so much that he was called "God's minstrel." His loving, Christlike ways inspired many others to join him in preaching and in serving in complete poverty. The order grew until it required extensive organization and rules that went beyond the Gospels' own instructions, complications that distressed Francis. He so meditated on Jesus that his body began to display the stigmata, the marks on hands, feet, and side of the crucified Christ. Recognizing that he was indeed a man of God, the sultan in Egypt listened to him preach. Though not converted from Islam, the Sultan granted priests in Jerusalem and Bethlehem concessions that the swords of the crusaders had failed to win.

Francis seems to have loved nature; legend says he preached to the birds. In his "Canticle of the Sun," still prayed by many, he praised God for "our brother the sun," for "our sister the moon," and for "our mother the earth." As his life neared its close he even praised the Lord for "our sister . . . death." The story of Francis has provided probably the best-loved model of Christ-likeness in all the history of the church.

Heretics

In part because of their new experiences with Eastern Orthodox Christians and with Muslim culture, Christians in central and western Europe began questioning traditional doctrines of Roman Catholicism. In southern Italy the Albigensian heretics made thousands of converts. Believing that the visible world is evil, the prison of souls, they denied that Christ had a body, and some taught that sinful souls might be reincarnated even as animals. The church set out to stop them, sincerely believing that it should not tolerate heresy. Salvation of one's soul depended on receiving the sacraments from the Roman Catholic Church and remaining faithful to it and its teachings. If killing the body was a crime, how much more heinous was the heretics' destruction of souls!

The church used three methods to win heretics back to orthodoxy. The Dominican friars served as a teaching arm of the church, attempting to persuade the heretics to return to Catholic doctrine. The church established the Inquisition, with judges to try heretics. The Inquisition was most active in the wealthiest areas, because the church could claim the property of convicted heretics, even property inherited from a heretic grandfather. Those arrested were not allowed to confront their accusers. Where persuasion failed, the Inquisition often resorted to torture. Many of those convicted were burned at the stake. There is no record of anyone ever having been acquitted. Where teaching and the Inquisition failed, the church had a third way, crusades against the heretics. Especially by that means the Albigensian heresy was eliminated. The church also attempted to convert Muslims, again using the sword to back up its demand for baptism.

The Inquisition became concerned for another group of "unbelievers," the Jews. Jews were alienated and persecuted in various ways. Some crusaders paused on their way to Palestine to slaughter them. Jews were often offered the choice of torture or baptism. Some might be arrested again if it was suspected that their conversion was insincere. In 1492, as Columbus was making his historic voyage, Spain was attempting to expel from its borders all unbaptized Jews.

Three heresies may be regarded as forerunners of the Protestant Reformation, those of Waldo, Wycliffe, and Hus. In the late twelfth century Peter Waldo had practiced and preached a life of poverty and of obedience to the Sermon on the Mount. He translated parts of the Bible from Latin into the language of the people and sent unordained preachers out to teach these Scriptures. The pope rejected his request for authorization, but he continued his work. Driven out of France into the Italian Alps, some of Waldo's followers survived persecution. These Waldensians preached doctrines so close to those taught centuries later by the Reformers that they eventually became part of the Presbyterian family of churches. Valdese, North Carolina, traces its heritage to Waldensian immigrants, and Waldensian churches continue in Italy.

In fourteenth-century England John Wycliffe, a professor at Oxford, attacked the idea that the church is the organization controlled by the hierarchy. His view was more like that of Augustine, who distinguished the existing Catholic Church from the kingdom of God. The church, he said, is not the hierarchy but all the elect, and the lives of many bishops and priests show that they are not of the elect. He protested the wealth of the church, which at that time owned about one-third of the land in England. In his day there were rival popes, each of whom said the other was damned. On that point, at least, Wycliffe agreed. The Bible, not the pope, should be the authority. Some of his disciples, later called Lollards, began traveling barefoot around England preaching his ideas. Most importantly, with the help of other scholars he began the first translation of the Bible out of Latin into English, the language of England's common people. His followers completed that work, made copies, and preached from it wherever they could. The church damned Wycliffe as roundly as he had damned the popes. He had to leave his post at Oxford and was for a while in prison. Protected by a wealthy nobleman, however, he was able to resume work as a parish priest, and at his death he was buried in consecrated ground. Thirty-one years later, however, the Council of Constance ordered his bones dug up, burned, and scattered in the river. Afraid of any translation brought out by a heretic and not under church auspices, and certainly not wanting it to substitute for papal authority, the church attempted to find and burn all copies of his English Bibles. His translation survived, however, and it became a model and ancestor for a succession of Bibles in English, down through the King James Version and its descendants even to the present day.

His influence spread to the Continent, where John Hus took up the cause. Like Wycliffe, Hus preached against the worldliness of the rival popes and many priests, argued that indulgences bring no forgiveness of sin, and wrote that the Bible should be the authority in the church. He was excommunicated and was forced to leave his position at the University of Prague, but he continued to write and to preach. The Council of Constance had been summoned in the hope of bringing some reforms to the church, and in 1415 Hus was ordered to appear before it. Though the emperor assured him that he would be kept in safety, he feared for his life, yet he resolved to go. Soon after his arrival he was arrested, and the emperor went back on his promise. Promises made to heretics were not valid, it was alleged. At length he was led in chains before the council. He promised to renounce any of his teachings that could be shown to be false, but the Bible should be the authority for such proof. That council had already ordered the burning of Wycliffe's bones, and Hus acknowledged that he approved of many of Wycliffe's teachings. Knowing that the council would condemn him, he affirmed, "I appeal to Jesus Christ, the only judge who is almighty and completely just. In his hand I place my cause." A month later he was taken back to the cathedral of Constance, clad in priestly robes. These were stripped off him, and his head was shaved and covered with a paper crown on which were pictures of demons. As he was led in chains to the stake he was taken past a bonfire of his books. Just before the fire around him was lighted he refused one last chance to recant. "Lord Jesus, it is for thee that I patiently endure this cruel death. I pray thee to have mercy on my enemies."[5]

Many were horrified by what the council had done, and Bohemian nationalism lent support to Hus's followers. Hundreds of noblemen assembled to announce their agreement with his doctrines, and a statement of four principles based on his teachings was adopted by various groups. Repeatedly the pope sent crusades to attack these rebellious Bohemians, and repeatedly the crusaders were defeated. At last a compromise was negotiated. Some followers of Hus,

especially in Moravia, rejected the compromise. At the time of the Reformation many made common cause with the Lutherans and experienced heavy
persecution from the Hapsburg emperors. Some allied with the Calvinists. In
the seventeenth century Bishop John Amos Comenius rallied Hussites.
Known as Moravians from their roots in Moravia, these pre-Reformation
Protestants continue today and are widely admired by others for their worldwide evangelistic mission work, their deeds of service, and their sometimes
costly witness in behalf of the cause of nonviolence and peace. In America
they early established settlements in Carolina and Pennsylvania.

The Renaissance

Though the church was opposed to heresies, it was not closed to all new ideas.
Monasteries had preserved learning throughout the so-called Dark Ages.
From the thirteenth century on, in many places in Europe there were great universities. It was the fourteenth and fifteen centuries, however, that saw the new
intellectual movement that is traditionally called the Renaissance, the rebirth.
Scholars took a new interest in the writers of ancient Greece and Rome.
Humanism focused not simply on God but also on humankind. The liberal arts
flourished. About 1450 Johannes Gutenberg invented the printing press, and
this was to help produce a cultural revolution. Now the works of scholars
could be disseminated and ancient manuscripts copied and preserved relatively free from error. The Latin Vulgate had been the only Scripture most
had previously known, but the new interest in ancient manuscripts brought a
new interest in the study of the Bible in its original languages of Greek and
Hebrew.

   The Renaissance church has given us great art. The great artists of Rome,
Florence, and other cities still pictured the Virgin, biblical scenes, and the
saints; but the men and women in Renaissance paintings looked far more
human, with feet more firmly planted on this earth, than did the stiff symbolic
figures produced by Gothic artists. Popes and the new wealthy merchant class
financed an unprecedented flowering of such art. Greek and Roman sculpture
provided stimulus for new work. The work of Michelangelo is symbolic of
the new era. His painting of the creation of Adam shows a giant but very
human-looking God reaching out to touch a perfect, muscular giant of a man.
His most famous sculpture was of David, a biblical hero, but it portrayed not
only piety toward God but the glory of the human body. Some painters began
depicting figures not just from the Bible but from ancient Greece and Rome

and included within biblical scenes portraits of the donors who had paid for their work.

Italy was the source of much of the new movement. In the fifteenth century wealthy families in Rome poured money into the arts. Popes brought great artists to Rome to adorn churches and palaces. Sometimes one family, such as the Borgias, dominated the papacy. Some popes publically acknowledged their concubines and their children, even though sometimes their mistresses were wives of others. High offices went to family members or were sold for huge prices. One wit said of Pope Alexander VI that he was ready to sell the keys of the kingdom, and that he had the right to do so because he had bought and paid for them himself.

Architects designed great palaces and cathedrals in forms quite different from the Gothic. So it came about that the largest, grandest, and most ornate of all churches should be built in Rome, the spiritual capital of the church. Saint Peter's, the Vatican, is still the destination of pilgrims from all over the world. To build such a church would cost an enormous amount of money. One way Pope Leo X undertook to raise such a sum was through the sale of indulgences.

In 1510 B. Giler of Kaiserberg preached before Emperor Maximilian:

> If the pope, the bishop, the emperor and the king do not reform our unspiritual, crazy, godless life, God will raise up a man to do it. I wish I might live to see the day and be his disciple, but I'm too old. But there are many of you here who will see and when that happens I bid you recall what I have said.[6]

Seven years after that prophecy, seeking to raise money for the construction of St. Peter's, one of Pope Leo's salesmen came to Wittenberg. Martin Luther posted a protest. The Protestant Reformation had begun.

Questions Chapter 4

1. What light does the story of the Crusades shed on contemporary conflicts between Muslim countries and the United States? What else can we learn from the Crusades' sad history?
2. What values and dangers do you see in having a pope who is the visible head and spokesperson for Christians?
3. The Inquisition was only one expression of the church's persecution of Jews. Protestants in Europe and in this country have discriminated against Jews, too. What is your church doing to help break down anti-Semitism in your community?

4. What hymns in your hymnal come from Bernard, Francis, or other medieval saints? Are there any plainsongs? What can we learn about Christian devotion from these musical gifts from the Middle Ages? from the great medieval cathedrals?
5. How was Protestantism foreshadowed by each of these pre-Reformation reformers: Peter Waldo? John Wycliffe? John Hus?
6. In summary, what gifts do we have from the church in this period? Why did the church need reforming, and how does it need reforming still?

Chapter 5

The Reformation on the Continent
(c. 1500–1700)

Each time a coin in the coffer rings
A soul from purgatory springs.[1]

*W*ith that singing commercial, accompanied by the beat of a drum and a
pompous parade, Dr. Johann Tetzel hawked indulgences in the university
town of Wittenberg, Germany. Of course, he could admit, you must be contrite concerning your sins, and you must confess them, but what way of showing contrition and of making confession could be better than securing an
indulgence? Repentance also requires doing good deeds to compensate for
your sins, and what better deed could you do than to contribute in this way to
building a new, monumental church over the bones of the chief of the apostles, Peter, at the Vatican in Rome!

Among those who were ready strongly to protest what seemed the sale of
God's grace was a thirty-four-year-old professor at the university, Martin Luther.

Luther's Early Life

His father used to beat him, and he says that one day a teacher caned him fifteen times because he was so slow in learning his Latin lessons. Nevertheless
Trebonius, one of his teachers, used to remove his hat as he greeted the class,
saying that these students were the poets and popes of the future. Martin Luther
was soon recognized as a brilliant student. He was also known for his singing.

His father reared him as a devout and orthodox Roman Catholic and wanted
young Martin to become a lawyer. Caught in a frightening storm, however, he
cried to St. Ann that he would become a monk; and so, to his father's distress,
he did. Luther did not do things halfway. "If ever a monk was saved by
monkery, it was I," he later sighed. Deeply concerned about his sins, he beat

himself, fasted, and once spent six hours confessing his transgressions. Finally the priest receiving his confession told him that if was going to spend that much time in confession he ought to go out and do something really worth confessing, like killing his father, rather than worrying so about the trivial sins about which he was so contrite. Jesus seemed to Luther a terrifying judge; he turned to the Virgin Mary for comfort.

He was sent on business to Rome, and there he availed himself of every opportunity to merit forgiveness. He climbed the holy stairs on his knees. He visited every church where indulgences were offered. He still felt himself a sinner. The luxury and worldliness of what was supposed to be the Holy City disillusioned him.

He had protested that it would kill him to become a professor, but that was the task appointed him. At first he taught philosophy as well as theology, but soon he began to concentrate on what became for the rest of his life his great love, the Bible. He wrote about the penitential psalms and lectured on Romans. It was in Galatians and Romans that he found what he had sought:

> Night and day I pondered until I saw the connections between the justice of God and the statement that "the just shall live by his faith" [Rom. 1:17]. Then I grasped that the justice of God is that righteousness by which through grace and sheer mercy God justifies us through faith. Thereupon I felt myself to be reborn and to have gone through open doors into paradise. The whole of Scripture took on a new meaning, and whereas before the "justice of God" had filled me with hate, now it became to be inexpressibly sweet in greater love. This passage of Paul became to me a gate to heaven.[2]

The Reformation Begins

There had been earlier reformers, and there were many forces, economic and political as well as theological, that produced the Protestant Reformation. Nevertheless, that Reformation is often said to have begun on October 31, 1517, when, protesting Tetzel's sale of indulgences, Martin Luther nailed his Ninety-five Theses to a kind of bulletin board, the door of the church at Wittenberg.

Bishop Albert wanted to add another see to his domain. For installing him, Pope Leo X wanted twelve thousand ducats, one thousand for each of the apostles. Albert offered seven, a thousand for each of the seven deadly sins. They compromised on ten. Albert had to borrow the money. The pope agreed to help him repay the loan through the sale of indulgences. Half the money would go to repay the loan, the other half to build St. Peter's Church. Tetzel, a scholarly and articulate traveling salesman, came to Wittenberg. Purchase an indulgence, he proclaimed, and you could secure forgiveness. You could do the same for relatives now languishing in purgatory and secure their release into heaven. Through the grace of God, baptism had erased their original sin, inherited from Adam, but the actual sins people had themselves committed required punishment or some balancing good deed. Now God graciously granted an opportunity to make atonement. What better deed could make up for one's sins than a gift to build the great new church? Tetzel was widely successful, but not with Luther.

Luther's Ninety-five Theses did not present his theology as it was to be developed later. He even found a place for indulgences in so far as they witnessed to the free grace of God. Thesis thirty-two expressed his dissent bluntly, "Those who believe that, through letters of pardon, they are made sure of their own salvation, will be eternally damned, along with their teachers." Though claiming that the pope agreed with him, it was on the basis of Scripture that Luther defended his attack. Tetzel made little attempt at scriptural defense but showed clearly that the pope approved what he was doing.

Luther came to regard the printing press as one of the great gifts of God. His theses were published and republished all over Europe. Other writings of Luther were published. Among the ideas in these writings, three gained emphasis: (1) The Scripture alone, not the bishops or even the pope, is to be our authority in faith and practice. (2) We are justified, made right with God, by grace received by faith alone. (3) All church members are called to be "priests" to one another, the keys to the kingdom being in the gospel granted to the whole community, not simply the hierarchy or the pope. The sale of indulgences seemed to Luther to offer salvation by good works, not by grace alone received by faith alone.

At first the pope made light of Luther's heresy, saying that this "drunken German" would change his mind when he sobered up. One reason why the pope hesitated before excommunicating Luther was that he did not want to alienate a number of the nobility who were delighted by a stand against the pope, because he drained so much money from their provinces. By 1520, however, the pope sent notice that Luther had sixty days in which to repent. Luther burned the papal bull (decree). A diet (court) of the empire convened early the next year at Worms. Luther was placed on trial. Shown some of his books, he readily agreed that he had written them, and others too. Asked to recant he replied:

Unless I am convicted by Scripture and plain reason—I do not accept the authority of pope and councils, for they have contradicted each other—my conscience is captive to the Word of God, I cannot and I will not recant anything, for to go against conscience is neither right nor safe. God help me. Amen.[3]

Excommunicated by the church and a fugitive from the state, Luther's life was in danger, but he had some powerful friends. Elector Frederick the Wise staged an apparent kidnaping and hid Luther in Wartburg castle. There Luther lived disguised as a knight, sometimes wearing armor. The battle he fought, however, was with his pen, for it was in his year at Wartburg that he produced his translation of the Bible into German. With the help of the printing press it was soon widely distributed and became the foundation of German-speaking Protestantism till this day. A year later, in spite of the threat to his life, he returned to Wittenberg. There he continued teaching and writing. He argued that there are only two sacraments, baptism and the Lord's Supper, these being instituted by Jesus Christ. Marriage, for example, one of the seven sacraments of the Catholic Church, was not a sacrament, since unions of Jews or of Muslins were valid marriages though not related to Christ. He rejected the doctrine of transubstantiation, the teaching that the bread and wine of the Lord's Supper are miraculously transformed into the body and blood of Christ. Rather, he said, Christ's body is "in, with, and under" the still material bread and wine. He had no intention of splitting the church or starting a new one. He wanted simply to remove from it those things that seemed to him contrary to Scripture, the one great authority.

He was still in many ways a medieval peasant, often using earthy language, though he was a master of German literature. He rivaled Catholics in damning the Jews. He refused compromise, even with Calvinists, on the doctrine of the Lord's Supper. Legend says that he had a stein on which was inscribed the Lord's Prayer. His friend the theologian Philipp Melanchthon could in one pull drink it down only to "forgive us our debts," but Luther could gulp it all the way to "Amen."

He heard that twelve girls in a nearby convent wanted to escape. His doctrine of the priesthood of all believers had led him to think that a housewife might be as holy as a nun. He plotted with a fishmonger. The covered wagon that brought the convent an order of fish left with twelve young women hidden where the fish had been. Luther now felt obligated to find them husbands. All went well except for Katie. The man Luther picked for her refused, saying Katie was not sufficiently aristocratic for him. Katie flatly refused to marry the next candidate. She confided to a friend to tell Dr. Luther that there were two men she would be willing to marry, one of whom was Luther himself. Martin and Katie were to set a pattern of married devotion. Jokingly he sometimes called her "my lord," and, punning on a German word, "my chain." They had six children and reared some others. Luther was one of the few leaders of the Reformation who has with other writings left us not only hymns, such as "A Mighty Fortress Is Our God," but also a cradle song. Not simply his thought and his translation of the Bible but his person influenced the spread of Lutheranism.

In 1530 Emperor Charles V, seeking to unite Germany against its enemies, requested a clear statement of Lutheran beliefs. Luther's friend Melanchthon wrote the first of the great Protestant confessions, the Augsburg Confession.

The concept of the separation of church and state had not yet been born. Thus inevitably the break with the pope meant a breakup of political alliances, and soon Germany was involved in religious wars. Luther himself did not believe in defending the gospel by means of violence, but his followers eventually formed armies. What seemed at the time the best compromise was that each state should follow the religion of its ruler. Some chose Rome, but many German states chose Lutheranism. That compromise did not always hold.

There were also Protestants in Germany who held to what came to be called Reformed theology, differing with the Lutherans primarily in relation to the Lord's Supper. In 1563, in Heidelberg, Germany, under the patronage of the elector Frederick, they adopted the Heidelberg Catechism, still beloved by millions of Presbyterians in many countries. Even more influential among many Presbyterians was the work of John Calvin in Geneva, Switzerland.

John Calvin and the Swiss Reformation

Sixteen years after Luther had nailed his Ninety-five Theses to the door of Wittenberg Cathedral, Nicolas Cop delivered his inaugural address as the newly elected rector of the University of Paris. Warned, he managed to escape just ahead of the police. His crime: he had championed the new Protestant heresy. Students now rushed with their warning to the home of his friend John Calvin, believed to be one from whom Cop had derived his unorthodox ideas. Legend says that they tied bed sheets together and let Calvin down out the back window while the police were knocking on his front door.

Born in 1509 in Noyon, France, Calvin had come to Paris to study law. He had become a friend of Cop and other humanists, and he had already published a book, a scholarly commentary on a work of the ancient Stoic philosopher Seneca. At some point, however, he experienced a conversion. "Like a flash of light, I realized in what an abyss of errors, in what chaos I was."[4] He turned from the study of law to the Scriptures, began to preach to congregations in the area, and started his career as a prolific writer expounding his Protestant ideas. Forced to flee Paris, he found refuge in the Swiss city of Basel, and there, at age twenty-seven, he completed the first edition of his most influential book, *The Institutes of the Christian Religion.* He was to produce many subsequent editions of the work, each expanding and building on the other. Luther was the pioneer of the Reformation, but Calvin was the one who most clearly systematized its doctrines.

He shared, defended, and developed Luther's belief in the sole authority of the Scriptures, in justification by grace received by faith alone, and in the priesthood of all believers. Calvin's starting point was the sovereignty of God. Almighty God, not the Roman Church with its sacraments, determines who will receive salvation. He is famous for his defense of the doctrine of predestination as presented by Paul in such passages as Romans 8:28–39 and 9:14–15, though he equally emphasized human responsibility for sin. Humankind had lost communion with God through its sin, he argued, becoming so bound to sin that in a sense even free will was lost. The justice of God demands that sin be punished. But Christ paid the price of sin, and now God's grace is freely given to all whom the sovereign God chooses. No one can take credit for the good one does or even for one's faith; they are gifts of God's grace. In many ways his thought was like that of Augustine. Perhaps some insight comes from words he was to speak on his deathbed: "I confess to live and die in this faith which He has given me, inasmuch as I have no other hope or refuge than His predestination upon which my entire salvation is grounded."[5] He could take no credit even for his faith; that too was entirely a gift of the gracious design of God (Eph. 2:8).

He found a larger place for the law than had Luther. The law convicts us of sin. As in gratitude the elect seek to do God's will, the moral law guides them. The state too should be guided by God's law. Thus political actions should reflect God's justice for all.

While Luther sought to remove from the church everything contrary to Scripture, Calvin went even further. His goal was to reform the church completely, in a sense to start over in the image of the New Testament church, including now only what was taught in Scripture. Thus Calvin favored a church government not by a pope but by a kind of democratic process, with church members electing elders who would rule, with trained pastors and teachers, a presbyterian system. He rejected holy days not based on Scripture, such as Christmas, Easter, and Lent, and instead stressed the Lord's Day, each week celebrating the resurrection. He differed with Luther also in the matter of the Lord's Supper. Lutherans held that the body of Christ was present "in, with, and under" the bread. The great Swiss reformer Huldrych Zwingli had proposed that the Lord's Supper was only a memorial to Christ's death. To Calvin the bread was still just bread; but, more than just a memorial, it was a symbol that lifted the believer's spirit to heaven where it fed truly, but spiritually, on the body of Christ. Luther had great admiration for his younger contemporary. Tragically, however, he would not agree to make common cause with the Swiss Reformation because his own view of the Lord's Supper seemed to him essential.

Calvin briefly returned to Paris to be with his former congregations, but once again he was forced into exile. On his way to Basel he spent the night at an inn in Geneva, where William Farel had already led in reformation. Farel pleaded with Calvin to stay and help complete the reformation there. Finally, when all his appeals had failed, the fiery, redheaded reformer made this solemn pronouncement: "You are concerned about your rest and your personal interests. . . . Therefore I proclaim to you in the name of Almighty God whose command you defy: Upon your work there shall rest no blessing. . . . Therefore let God damn your rest, let God damn your work!" Apparently fearing Farel's curse, Calvin submitted. "I obey God."[6] Calvin stayed in Geneva the rest of his life, except for three years when opponents so rebelled at his strictness that they exiled him.

The "Libertines," opponents of Calvin's efforts to enforce strict morality, had reason to resent his reforms. Calvin expected the city council to pass and enforce laws in accord with the Word of God as he understood it. The instigator of an indecent performance was made to do public penance, kneeling in the cathedral. The owner of a gambling house was put in the pillory for an hour, wearing a necklace of cards. A perjurer was displayed on a ladder, the right hand with which he had sworn falsely tied above him. An adulterous couple was led through the streets in disgrace. Parents who refused to send their children to school were fined. Councilmen themselves might be punished for offenses.[7]

In the next election the party of the Libertines gained the majority. They too, however, attempted to enforce order, but rebellion broke out. Eventually the council decided to remove Farel and Calvin from the pulpit. They refused to obey. That night there was a riot. Men pounded on Calvin's door and threw rocks at his house. He reports that he heard at least sixty gunshots. Someone shouted a demand that he be thrown into the river as a traitor. Yet the next day he ascended into the pulpit to preach. The afternoon service ended in a riot, including sword fights. The council expelled Calvin and Farel.

Calvin spent three years in exile in Strasbourg, peacefully preaching, teaching, and writing. Three years later a new council recognized Geneva's need, and reluctantly he agreed to return.

Though always sickly, Calvin led an amazingly busy life. He preached every Sunday, every other week conducted the weekday services, and lectured three times a week. More than two thousand of his sermons have been preserved. He wrote commentaries on almost every book of the Bible except Revelation. (He admitted that he did not understand that one.) He carried on correspondence with church leaders of various persuasions all over Europe. He once said that he would cross every sea if by doing so he could reunite the church. He wrote books circulated throughout Europe. He visited the sick. He met with the church elders once a week. Repeatedly he urged the city council to push for some law or its enforcement. He helped to bring new industry to the city and once served as an official diplomat to another city-state. He urged that education be offered to all. He worked for a plan for public health. He was a most important leader in the development of a great university at Geneva. At the same time he was for eight years a family man. After bearing him three children, each of whom died early, his beloved wife also died.

Intertwined with Calvin's good activities was one which, centuries later, Calvinists deplore. The concept of religious liberty and the separation of church and state had not yet been born. Thus he expected the council to pass laws in accordance with Scripture and to punish crimes that seemed contrary to the true faith. There was probably more freedom of religion in Calvin's Geneva than in almost any other city of Europe. The infamous tragedy of Calvin's ministry is that during his time at Geneva Michael Servetus was burned at the stake. Servetus, who questioned the doctrine of the Trinity, had been condemned to the flames in a Catholic city, Lyon, and had escaped to Geneva. There, apparently, he hoped to replace Calvin as its spiritual leader. He was arrested. Calvin acceded to the city council's death penalty but pleaded with them, to no avail, for a more humane form of execution. Today at the spot where Servetus was burned a monument has been erected by Calvin's followers expressing repentance.

Geneva attracted not only exiles like Servetus but also students from all over Europe, who came to Geneva to study under Calvin. Soon his ideas were being spread to churches all over Britain and the Continent.

Even a bit earlier than Luther or Calvin, Zwingli had independently arrived at a Protestant theology much like that of Calvin. In 1566 his successor as pastor in Zurich, Heinrich Bullinger, penned the Second Helvetic Confession, the earliest of the Reformed creeds that have continued through the centuries to define the faith of Presbyterians.

The Reformation in France

In 1950 a visitor in a Protestant (Reformed) Church in France noticed a plaque on the wall. "Are those the names of members of your congregation who died in the war?" he asked. "Oh, no," his host replied. "These are members of this congregation who were martyrs for our faith." Protestantism in France produced many martyrs.

Calvin wrote not only in Latin but in French, and his ideas spread rapidly in his native land. Especially in the south of France and among the better educated, the professional and artisan people, Protestantism took root. By 1559 a national synod was held in Paris, adopting a presbyterian form of government and a creed reflecting Calvin's theology. French Protestants became known as Huguenots. One estimate is that at their high point there were as many as four hundred thousand Protestants in France. Their growing number, with their democratic church government, was seen as a political threat to the powerful and militantly Catholic Guise family. In fact the first duke of Guise was assassinated by a Protestant. In 1562 the duke of Guise's troops attacked a Protestant church service at Vassy and slaughtered its men, women, and children. Off and on for more than a century France was involved in religious war. At times the Protestants won some degree of freedom. Visitors to the Louvre in Paris may see across the street a statue to Gaspard de Coligny, an outstanding Protestant leader. An attempt to assassinate Coligny produced angry reaction from Protestants. Catherine de Medici persuaded her son, King Charles IX, that the Huguenots were a threat to his reign—a threat that required drastic action. On the eve of St. Bartholomew's Day, 1572, the royal army hunted down and slaughtered three thousand Protestants in Paris. Within three days twenty thousand more in the rest of France were hunted down and executed. Pope Gregory XIII struck a medal to commemorate the occasion. Philip II of Spain joined in the effort to kill all Protestants. Thousands more were executed. Thousands fled to Switzerland, Holland, and England, and eventually some even crossed the ocean to America.

There were, however, French Catholics who were horrified by this violence. A fanatical Dominical friar, distressed by the relatively tolerant policies of King Henry III, assassinated that monarch, and his cousin, Henry IV, fell heir to the throne. He was at least nominally a Protestant, but he recognized that his religion would be an obstacle to his ruling Catholic France. "Paris is worth a mass," he decided, and he converted to Catholicism. He did, however, try to bring peace between the warring factions, in 1598 proclaiming some degree of tolerance with the Edict of Nantes.

In 1685 Louis IV revoked that edict. Bloody war almost exterminated French Protestantism, but a remnant survived as an illegal religion. At last the French Revolution brought them freedom, and the Reformed Church continues to preach and practice the gospel in many French communities.

The Reformation in Holland

Protestantism and freedom from Spanish rule were twin causes in the Dutch revolution. Philip II of Spain, a sincerely devout Roman Catholic, was determined to keep his Dutch provinces true to the ancestral faith. When a Dutch ambassador come to plead for mercy for the Netherlands, Philip knelt before his crucifix and prayed: "Almighty God, I beseech thee that I may be saved from ruling over a people that deny thee." He then rose and announced that he would rather lose one hundred thousand lives than change even one of his edicts against the Protestants. Their devotion matched his. One hundred thousand is often given as the number of Dutch Protestants who died fighting for Calvinism and independence. Thus Holland had more martyrs than any other country. Perhaps as many as one hundred thousand families fled Holland to other countries to escape from the Catholic Inquisition. Some settled in America. (New York was originally New Amsterdam, named by Dutch settlers for the Dutch capital.)

Political independence was by no means the Dutch Protestants' only concern. They were committed to Reformed doctrine, especially as presented in the Heidelberg Catechism.

Among the Spanish king's diplomats was William of Orange, whose taciturn manner earned him the title "William the Silent." Though born to Dutch Lutheran parents, William was reared a Roman Catholic. When the Spanish Inquisition began torturing and executing Protestants, William rebelled. He was perhaps never a really devout Calvinist; with four wives he rivaled England's Henry VIII. He did, however, become at least nominally a Calvinist, and behind him the Presbyterian Dutch rallied for freedom. Spain was probably the mightiest empire in Europe. Little Holland was greatly outnumbered. But such was their devotion to Protestantism and to political freedom that in the end they were victorious.

On the statue to William the Silent in New Brunswick, New Jersey, is this inscription: "As long as he lived he was the guiding star of a brave nation, and when he died the little children cried."

Having thrown off the oppression of the Roman Catholics, the Dutch Calvinists sometimes became oppressors themselves, often persecuting Jews and other Christians. Nevertheless, they offered more freedom of religion than most countries of Europe. It was to Holland that the Pilgrims were to flee before going to America. Another of Holland's great gifts to the world is the art of a devout, highly independent Protestant, Rembrandt van Rijn.

Anabaptists, the Left Wing of the Reformation

At various places in Europe there appeared Christians who felt that the Reformers had not gone far enough. Rebelling against the Roman Catholic doctrine that seemed to guarantee salvation to every person who had been baptized in infancy, they rejected the whole practice of infant baptism. In the New Testament, they argued, it is only those old enough to choose to believe who are baptized. They began to baptize one another as adults, even though they had been baptized in infancy, and thus they came to be called "Anabaptists," or "those who baptize again." Some began to practice baptism by immersion.

One of their first preachers was Conrad Grebel. Converted in Zurich under the preaching of the Presbyterian pioneer Zwingli, he began to preach that the church needed to go further. He organized small study groups—often potentially explosive organizations. In a big debate over his proposals before the city council, Zwingli was adjudged to have won, and Grebel's study groups were outlawed. They continued, however, in secret. Grebel was sentenced to life imprisonment on a diet of bread, gruel, and water, but he escaped and spread Anabaptist doctrines wherever he could.

Zwingli believed in letting the punishment fit the crime: since they were so concerned about water, drown these heretics! Anabaptist Feliz Manz, for example, was doubled up and bound, then thrown into the river. His final cry was, like that of Jesus, "Into thy hands I commend my spirit."

John Christian Wenger discusses the differences between typical early Anabaptists and Zwingli's Presbyterians:

Zwingli	Anabaptists
state church	free church
enforced doctrine	religious liberty
oaths permitted	oaths forbidden
infant baptism	baptism of believers only
love and nonresistance an ideal	literal pacifism
church involved in social concerns	withdrawal from all political activity[8]

In Münster, Germany, a fanatical group of Anabaptists formed a kind of commune, banished or executed all who refused adult baptism, and instituted polygamy. The Anabaptist movement in many places, however, developed responsible leadership, and became the ancestors of several enduring groups. The Mennonites and the Quakers preserved the Anabaptist emphasis on peace and love. The Amish demonstrated their courage to be different. Later some other groups who rejected infant baptism called themselves simply "Baptists." They were to became a major force for Christianity in many places, especially in America.

The Right Wing of the Reformation: The Counter-Reformation

Catholicism's first reaction to Luther proved futile. Pope Leo X appointed a new general of the Augustinian order to "quench a monk of his order, Martin Luther by name, and thus smother the fire before it should became a world conflagration."

Other reactions, however, produced saints. Commandos in the Catholic war for souls were the Jesuits, headed by a contemporary of Calvin named Ignatius Loyola. He had been a soldier, fighting for the queen of Spain against the French. Now he would be a knight for the Queen of Heaven, Mary, fighting against Protestantism.

In Palestine one dark night he crept past Muslim guards, ascended the Mount of Olives, and planted his own feet in the footprints of Jesus that legend said were preserved there. It was a symbol of his determination to follow Jesus. All Christians might well pray his prayer: "Take, O Lord, and receive all my liberty, my memory, my understanding, and all my will, all I have and possess. You have given it to me. To You, Lord, I return it. All is Yours. Dispose of it entirely according to Your will. Give me Your love and grace because that is enough for me." For Loyola complete dedication to God required complete dedication to the pope. The Jesuits became leaders of the Inquisition. Jesuit missionaries spread their understanding of the gospel to India, China, and even Japan. In France Jesuit Vincent de Paul set out to help the poor, the imprisoned, and especially the sick. In those days before Florence Nightingale the hospitals were worse than the diseases. He and Louise de Marillac began to enlist young women as nurses, a relatively unheard-of thing in that day. Eventually they became known as the Daughters of Charity. Jesuits led in the efforts to destroy the Protestant "heresy."

Stimulated in part by the Reformation, the Catholic Church made many reforms in disciplining and educating its priests, and it began to display new vigor. One party, led by Cardinal Contarini, was concerned primarily for moral reform and might even have been willing to accept Luther's idea of justification by faith. His opponent, Caraffa, however, was as strict doctrinally as morally. It was Caraffa who became Pope Paul IV and made himself chief inquisitor.

Reforms were instituted at the Council of Trent, but not reforms of doctrine. Among its decrees were these: "If anyone says that . . . faith alone . . .

suffices for obtaining grace, let him be anathema." If anyone denies the doctrine of "transubstantiation," that the bread of the mass "is converted into the
substance of the body of Christ . . . let him to be anathema . . . If anyone shall
say that the sacrifice of the mass . . . ought not to be offered for the living and
the dead . . . let him be anathema."[9]

"Anathema" means "damned."

Hatred and Hope

Hatred of false teachings led to hatred of those who taught them. This hatred
allied itself with political ambitions. The result was the Thirty Years War
(roughly 1618–1648). Protestant states fought Catholic states. But soon the
religious element was almost forgotten in the nationalist rivalries of the time,
so that sometimes men fought others of the same faith. Almost every country
in Europe was involved. An estimated three hundred thousand were killed in
battle. Germany suffered most. One estimate is that its population declined in
those thirty years from twenty-one million to less that fourteen million. Such
slaughter was a kind of preview of the twentieth century's two world wars.

Popes cried anathemas against Protestants and Protestants damned the
pope as the antichrist. But we should remember that there was also deep devotion to the Prince of Peace. A discussion of the Reformation should include
some examples of prayer and devotion. Here are three. Martin Luther sang
this prayer:

> From depths of woe I cry to Thee,
> Lord, hear me, I implore Thee,
> Bend down Thy gracious ear to me,
> My prayer let come before Thee.
> If thou rememberest each misdeed,
> If each should have its rightful meed,
> What may abide Thy presence?
>
> Thy love and grace alone avail
> To blot out my transgression;
> . . . .
> Therefore my hope is in the Lord
> And not in mine own merit;
> It rests upon His faithful Word
> To them of contrite spirit.
> . . . .

And though it tarry till the night
And till the morning waken,
My heart shall never doubt His might
Nor count itself forsaken.[10]

John Calvin prayed:

Grant, Almighty God, that, since to a perverse, and in every way a rebellious people, thou didst formerly show so much grace, as to exhort them continually to repentance, and to stretch forth thy hand to them by thy Prophets—O grant, that the same word may sound in our ears; and when we do not immediately profit by thy teaching, O cast us not away, but by thy Spirit, so subdue all our thoughts and affections, that we, being humble, may give glory to thy majesty, such as is due to thee, and that being allured by thy paternal favor, we my submit ourselves to thee, and at the same time, embrace that mercy which thou offerest and presentest to us in Christ, that we may not doubt but thou wilt be a Father to us, until we shall at length enjoy that eternal inheritance, which has been obtained for us by the blood of thine only-begotten Son. Amen.[11]

Finally, here are words from the saintly Teresa of Avila, suitable for students of history:

We need to cultivate, and think upon, and seek the companionship of those who, through living on earth like ourselves, have accomplished such great deeds for God; the last thing we should do is to withdraw of set purpose from our greatest help and blessing, which is the most sacred Humanity of Our Lord Jesus Christ. . . . for, if they lose the Guide, the good Jesus, they will be unable to find their way; they will do well if they are able to remain securely in other Mansions. For the Lord Himself says that He is the Way. . . . For life is long and there are many trials in it and we have need to look at Christ our Pattern, and also at His Apostles and Saints, and reflect how they bore these trials, so that we too may bear them perfectly. The good Jesus is too good company for us to forsake Him.[12]

Questions Chapter 5

1. Surveys show that the majority of Americans assent to propositions such as the following: "The just God will reward you depending on whether you are good or bad." How would Luther respond? What does the "justice" or "righteousness" of God mean, according to a favorite text of Luther, Rom. 1:17?

2. This chapter describes three emphases of Luther. Be sure you know them! How are they basic to Protestant understanding of Christian doctrine?
3. How did Calvin expand, clarify, and add to the doctrines first proposed by Luther? How are his ideas echoed in our confessions of faith today?
4. How does your church's Presbyterian government reflect New Testament principles and the work of Calvin? What other gifts have come to our church and nation from our heritage from Calvin?
5. Why may Protestants of French and Dutch descent glory in their heritage? Recall also the Heidelberg Catechism, which comes from Reformed thinkers in Germany.
6. In what ways did the Counter-Reformation bring needed changes in the Roman Church itself? How did Catholicism harden its stand against some Presbyterian doctrines?

Chapter 6

The Reformation in Great Britain
(c. 1500–1700)

*M*issionaries, refugees, adventurers, and other immigrants were to bring Protestantism and Roman Catholicism to many lands, enriching all of them with the gospel in its many different forms. For the thirteen colonies that were to become the United States of America, however, it was the Protestant Reformation in England and Scotland that proved most influential.

Henry VIII

"Luther wanted to get married. Henry VIII wanted to get divorced." The first half of that alleged explanation of the Reformation is completely false. There is no hint anywhere that Luther had any thought of marriage when he posted his Ninety-five Theses, bore his witness at Worms, and translated the Bible. It is quite true that Henry wanted a new wife.

The roots of genuine Protestantism in England, however, were much deeper. In the fourteenth century John Wycliffe had led in reforms. In the sixteenth century he was still remembered, and in spite of efforts to stamp out his movement there were still some of his followers (called "Lollards") in England and Scotland. More importantly, four years before Henry VIII broke with the pope, William Tyndale had published his translation, influenced by Wycliffe, rendering the New Testament into contemporary English. A scholar, Tyndale translated Scripture not from the official Latin Vulgate but from the original Greek. Shunned by Cuthbert Turnstall, the bishop of London, he found a merchant who would house him, and very quietly he continued his work. Soon, however, he was forced to flee to Luther's Germany. Even there his life was in danger, but for a while he seemed safe in Worms. There he entered into the smuggling business. He bootlegged Bibles into Britain under bales of cloth, in sacks of flour, and in any other way that would get them past

the authorities. Bishop Turnstall seemed unable to stop these illegal ship-
ments, so, at the suggestion of someone who was secretly a sympathizer with
Tyndale, the bishop decided on a new plan: he would buy all the Bibles he
could find as they arrived, then destroy them. Now money poured in. Tyndale
promptly used this new wealth to print more Bibles and to smuggle in hundreds more, financed by his enemy, the bishop of London. Too late, the church
realized its mistake and began simply preaching against the translation, alleg-
ing that is was full of errors. There were errors, but Tyndale worked hard to
correct them in new editions. At length a henchman of Bishop Thomas More
enticed Tyndale to venture out of the town, where he could be safely arrested.
He spent many months in a cold prison. In one letter he begged a friend to
intercede for him to be allowed to get his warmer coat and a hat. Instead, he
was tied to a stake and strangled to death, and his body was burned. His dying
words were, "Lord, open the king of England's eyes!" Three years later his
prayer was answered; Henry himself authorized the translation and publication of a Bible in English.

Henry was never a very good Protestant. Earlier he had published an essay
denouncing Luther, and Pope Leo X had rewarded Henry with the title
"Defender of the Faith." (British monarchs still use that title.) It was not so
much from lust that Henry determined to get a younger wife. In all likelihood
he satisfied his sexual appetite outside marriage. What seemed crucial was
that a wife provide the king a male heir. Catherine had borne him five children, but only one had survived, the girl Mary, whom Protestants would later
call "Bloody Mary." Henry and his subjects believed that the security of the
nation would be threatened if he did not produce a son to inherit the throne.
Perhaps in part for fear of antagonizing Catherine's family, on the throne in
powerful Spain, the pope refused an annulment of Henry's marriage. Thomas
Cranmer, however, claimed that Henry had scriptural grounds to believe his
marriage was invalid, and, making provision for her, Henry set Catherine
aside. The pope excommunicated Henry.

Most of England had little love for the pope anyway; for years too much
money, they thought, had been going to Rome. Henry declared himself to be
head of the Church of England, closed monasteries, and began confiscating
church property. (The church had owned perhaps one-third of the lands in
England.) In many respects the church he headed was little different from that
of Rome. For example, indulgences were still sold. For a lesser sin you paid
ten shillings. But eating meat on a fast day cost you forty. He did, however,
authorize a prayerbook in English, edited by Cranmer, now Archbishop of
Canterbury. In 1539 he authorized an official translation of the Bible, based
largely on Tyndale's work. It was to be placed in every church. Its first page

contained a picture of Henry himself, kneeling in prayer. The Reformation in England had begun.

Edward and Mary

Under Henry's son Edward, who inherited the throne as a boy only nine years old, the Church of England became more truly Protestant. Cranmer persuaded Parliament to adopt what became Forty-two Articles of the faith for the English churches, later revised to Thirty-nine. Among those who advised in that process was a Scots Protestant named John Knox, who served briefly as one of the king's chaplains. More importantly, Cranmer completed an early form of the Prayer Book, including in it mostly material from Catholic sources but with Protestant selection and additions. Its use was now required in all churches in England. The Prayer Book became the basis of Anglican worship, and of the worship in Episcopal churches throughout the world. Christians of many other denominations have used its beautifully worded prayers. It has been the Book of Common Prayer more than the doctrines of the Thirty-nine Articles that has molded the Anglican Church. These prayers were in English, not Rome's Latin. Priests were allowed to marry. Whereas the laypeople had been allowed to take only the bread at the Lord's Supper, now they also were given the cup. Protestant publications and preaching spread throughout the nation. Political leaders saw Protestantism as a bulwark against encroachments by England's great enemy, loyally Roman Catholic Spain.

After only six years, however, the frail boy king died. A coup to place on the throne the king's Protestant cousin Lady Jane Grey failed, and Henry the Eighth's firstborn began her reign. Descended from Spanish kings and now the bride-to-be of the heir to the throne of Catholic Spain, she would live to be dubbed by Protestants "Bloody Mary."

Mary had reason to hate Protestants. Her father, Henry VIII, had broken with the pope in order to set aside her mother. Protestants like Cranmer had declared her parents' marriage invalid; thus Protestants had proclaimed her a bastard. She had been reared a devout Catholic. And her family ties and a major source of her security lay with staunchly Roman Catholic Spain, enemy of England's Protestant partisans. A year after taking the throne she married the heir to the Spanish empire. Parliament declared that, after all, the pope really is the head of the church.

Among the many Protestant leaders who fled the country was the fiery John Knox. In the spirit of the Old Testament prophets, he predicted that God's judgment would now visit England with plagues, famine, and mass rape of its women. That did not occur; instead, a year and a half after Mary became queen she was sufficiently entrenched that she could order John Rogers burned at the stake, England's first Protestant martyr under its new ruler.

Fearing, with reason, that a Protestant plot might depose her and put her half-sister Elizabeth on the throne, she sent that future queen to the Tower of London, though after three months she released her to a kind of house arrest. Compared with rulers on the Continent, Mary's policy was moderate; in all she had probably less than three hundred Protestants burned as heretics and traitors. Archbishop Cranmer accepted the rule of his new sovereign and at royal command even signed a statement acceding to papal authority, but it did not save him. Overcome with guilt for that moment of cowardice in signing documents he knew to be false, at his execution he deliberately held out to be burned first his hand that had signed his recantation.

Of the nearly three hundred who were burned, it was former bishops Hugh Latimer and Nicholas Ridley whose martyrdom most stirred the English Protestants. Weeping crowds watched as the faggots were lit around them. For centuries Protestants have recalled Latimer's words as the fire rose. "Be of good comfort, Mr. Ridley, and play the man! We shall this day light such a candle, by God's grace, in England, as I trust shall never be put out."[1]

His prophecy was more accurate than that of John Knox. Thousands who had not greatly cared whether England was Protestant or Catholic were horrified by Mary's executions and began to identify with Protestantism. Thus the way was prepared when Mary died after a reign of only five years, and the Protestant Elizabeth inherited the throne.

Queen Elizabeth I

With Elizabeth on the throne, those who had fled Mary began returning. "The wolves," Bishop White exclaimed, "are coming out of Geneva . . . and hath sent their books before, full of pestilent doctrines, blasphemy, and heresy."[2] That Catholic bishop had reason to be afraid. There were to be Roman Catholic martyrs now. Centuries later many Protestants sing the hymn "Faith of Our Fathers," recalling "our fathers, chained in prisons dark." Most are quite unaware that one stanza of the original version expressed its author's trust: "Faith of our fathers, Mary's prayers / Will win all England back to thee." A kind of Catholic underground network attempted to provide shelter and even disguises for traveling priests. In some old British houses one may still see "priest holes," secret chambers where devout Catholics risked their lives to hide itinerant priests from Protestant persecutors.

Elizabeth was surely one of the most remarkable women in history. She was a brilliant scholar, fluent in several of the languages of the Continent, able to carry on a conversation in Latin, and given to reading the New Testament in the original Greek. A beautiful twenty-five-year-old as she began her reign, she used her diplomatic skill and sexual charm to balance off France and Spain, teasing each with the possibility of sharing her throne through marriage. She inherited a little island torn by strife within and facing powerful enemies abroad. Yet for forty-five years she ruled with a strong hand and laid the foundations for a mighty empire.

It was inevitable that she would reign as a Protestant. When Henry had married her mother Anne Boleyn, the pope had declared her mother a whore and Elizabeth a bastard. She was aware that some who were loyal to the pope plotted to replace her on the throne with her Catholic cousin, Mary, Queen of Scots.

Elizabeth's great concern, however, was not to support Protestantism or Catholicism. What she wanted was religious unity in the nation, with herself as earthly head of the church. She undertook to secure this conformity in two ways. "No bishop, no prince," she believed; therefore she appointed bishops, loyal to her rather than to the pope. And she decreed that the official Prayer Book should be used in every church. In spite of doctrinal differences, she hoped, both Catholics and Protestants could conform to the use of the Book of Common Prayer and the authority of the bishops in one great Church of England.

Puritans and Separatists

For most people her compromise worked well. There were, however, Catholics who worshiped in secret and plotted her overthrow. And a growing number of Protestants felt Elizabeth's reforms had not gone nearly far enough. Seeking to purify the church, they became known as "Puritans."

Supported by the state and by private endowments, many of the clergy of England were unfit for their duties. Puritans in one county protested to Parliament such priests as these:

> Mr. Levit . . . a notorious swearer, a dicer, a carder . . . he hath a childe by a maid.
> James Allen . . . unable to preach.
> Mr. Phippe . . . convicted of whoredome . . . unable to preach.
> Mr. Atkins . . . thrice presented for a drunkard.
> Mr. Ampleforth . . . Hath a childe by his owne sister.[3]

The Puritans' concern was not only about the ignorance and immorality of the clergy; they had doctrinal problems with Elizabeth's church too. Many of the Protestants who had fled from Mary had been influenced by the teachings of the Calvinists they encountered on the Continent. Puritans loved to publish their views, and they circulated their Calvinist tracts widely. The Calvinistic ideal was to restore the church to its New Testament pattern. Did the disciples kneel at the Last Supper? No, they protested. Kneeling at the Eucharist had come about in Catholicism's adoration of the bread as the transubstantiated body of Christ. Hence Puritans opposed kneeling. The apostles did not wear elaborate vestments, and so some Puritan pastors would not do so either. Some began to preach that church government by bishops was contrary to the New Testament. As for the Prayer Book, there were Calvinists who wanted something more completely in accord with Geneva and regarded it as bits "plucked out of that popish dunghill, the mass book." They looked with envy to Scotland, where a presbyterian system of leaders elected by the laity was taking hold. Elizabeth saw clearly that such a democratic system "consorted not at all with monarchy." Five who worked to get Parliament to adopt the presbyterian system Elizabeth promptly jailed in the Tower.

The majority of Puritans remained loyal, but Elizabeth sensed a threat to her rule. To enforce uniformity she decreed that if for four weeks you failed to attend the Church of England with its Prayer Book liturgy you could be arrested and remain in jail until you recanted. If you missed for three months you were to be deported. If you returned to England you would be executed. Puritan ministers who dispensed with the Prayer Book had to change their minds or lose their churches. In 1593 the Welsh pamphleteer John Penry was hanged for espousing the Puritans' heretical views.

Puritans came to think of the church not as the society at prayer but as a covenant fellowship, called from the world to be saints. They were to show that they were truly elect by living godly lives; those who were most evidently sinners might be barred from the Lord's Table.

A minority simply could not compromise and would not remain loyal to the Church of England. Separating, they formed their own groups, electing their own pastors. These Separatists sometimes felt they must separate even from one another. One extreme case illustrates their—usually much more rational—rejection of worldly living. Thomasine, wife of Thomas Johnson, a Separatist pastor, was accused by Thomas's brother George of, among other things:

> wearing of a long busk [corset] after the fashion of the world. . . . Whalebones in the bodies of peticotes . . . against nature. . . . Great sleeves sett out with whalebones. . . . She stoode gazing, bracing or vaunting in shop doores. . . . She laide in bedd on the Lordes day till 9 a clock . . . she being not sick.[4]

The two brothers were in prison for their beliefs at the time. Eventually the accuser was excommunicated. He wrote a 215-page book about the affair, and their congregation, exiled to Holland, split. This, I must repeat, was an extreme example, but Separatists and their more moderate Puritan sisters and brothers did place great emphasis on godly living,

Several of the Separatist groups fled England to Holland. The most celebrated of these left Holland for the New World and founded the Plymouth Colony.[5] The group with millions of more direct descendants today, however, is that which followed John Smythe (or Smyth) to Holland. Smythe, a priest of the Church of England and a teacher at Cambridge, began to differ so strongly with what he regarded as the errors of the church that he finally felt it necessary to leave England with a group of disciples. Influenced in part by some Mennonites, Smythe was convinced that infant baptism was invalid and that baptism was for believers only; so he baptized himself and then the members of his congregation. Thus they become the first English-speaking Baptists. Smythe, however, moved further from traditional practices, even rejecting from worship services all but spontaneous singing and praying. He even forbade the reading of the Bible in translation during worship, since no translation was the original Word of God. He left the group he had founded.

Associated with Smythe at first was Thomas Helwys. In 1611 he led a group back to England, and there they became the first Baptist congregation on English soil. Smythe had practiced baptism by sprinkling or pouring, but Helwys became convinced that the New Testament practice was immersion. Helwys has another distinction: he wrote the first essay in English defending the idea of religious toleration. It is part of the glory of the Baptist heritage that through the centuries Baptists, more consistently than almost any others, Protestant or Catholic, have advocated the separation of church and state.

In England the Baptists were to multiply rapidly in spite of many being thrown into prison. English Baptists boast such converts as Isaac Newton and John Bunyan, who in prison wrote *Pilgrim's Progress*. Baptists served with Presbyterians and other Puritans in the army of Cromwell when Charles II was overthrown and the Protectorate established.

John Knox and the Beginning of the Reformation in Scotland

More than to any other, the Reformation in Scotland owed its success to the chaplain of a group of assassins, the fiery John Knox. Knox remains a controversial figure. Edwin Muir could find in his 315-page biography little to praise about this reformer.

> What Knox really did was to rob Scotland of all the benefits of the Renaissance. Scotland never enjoyed these as England did, and no doubt the lack of that immense advantage has had a permanent effect. It can be felt, I imagine, even at the present day.[6]

By contrast, Presbyterian historian A. Mervyn Davies suggests that in Knox's contest with Mary, Queen of Scots, not only the fate of Protestantism but "the fate of the whole world, and particularly the fate of our nation still to be born, rested on the shoulders of this one man."[7] He credits the church for which Knox crusaded with being the major force in establishing not only Protestantism but both democracy and education in Scotland and then in America.

The Protestant assassins with whom Knox soon allied himself had not struck the first blow. In 1545 at the university town of St. Andrews, George Wishart, preacher of the new Protestant heresy, was burned at the stake. A few days later sixteen young upper-class Scots broke into St. Andrews Castle and stabbed Catholic Cardinal Beaton to death.

Knox, a thirty-one-year-old Catholic priest, had been a tutor to sons of Scots lords. Moved by Wishart's preaching, he had served as a guard for the reformer, carrying a sword to protect Wishart from the expected arrest. Wishart, however, became resigned to martyrdom and dismissed his guard: "One life is enough for a sacrifice. Gang back to your bairns, Maister Knox, and God bless you!" Though probably not personally involved in the vengeful assassination of Cardinal Beaton, soon after that crime Knox did join the conspirators, entrenched at St. Andrews Castle. There a Protestant garrison held out against troops of Scotland and its French ally and surrendered only when a treaty was reached. The assassins, including Knox, were promised to be deported to France but then freed to go wherever they wished. The promise proved to be a lie. Instead, for the next nineteen months Knox was chained to an oar and forced to row as a galley slave in a French naval vessel.

Once from their boat the galley slaves caught a glimpse of St. Andrews. To a fellow slave Knox boldly prophesied that one day he would again preach in St. Andrews Church.

It was probably through negotiation by the English court that Knox was released. Bishop Cranmer welcomed him to England, and there he served until King Edward was succeeded by Mary. Made one of King Edward's chaplains, he helped prepare the document that became the Thirty-nine Articles of the Church of England. He refused, however, to accept the office of bishop. When "Bloody Mary" became queen, Knox fled to France.

Never a diplomat, Knox seemed often to dip his pen in acid. Mary, of the Guise family that had persecuted Huguenots in France, was now ruling in Scotland as regent for her child, Mary, Queen of Scots. Attacking her and Catholic Queen Mary in England, Knox sent back to England and Scotland his *First Blast of the Trumpet against the Monstrous Regiment of Women*. In other writings Knox compared Mary of England to Old Testament Jezebel and recalled pointedly that Jehu had violently rid Israel of that queen.

The exiled Knox found a home in John Calvin's Geneva. It was, he wrote, the most perfect school of Christ since the days of the apostles. There he became the pastor of a congregation of English refugees. When Elizabeth succeeded to the throne, many of these returned to England and spread the Calvinist doctrines that nurtured Puritanism.

Knox returned to Scotland in 1559, determined to make Scotland a Presbyterian nation. By the standards of the time, Regent Mary of Guise was quite restrained and tolerant, but she was clearly committed to Roman Catholicism. Knox's return was accompanied by riots. Monasteries were burned, images and stained-glass windows destroyed, and churches looted. Knox did not approve such vandalism, but he made no real attempt to stop it. He went here and there preaching denunciations of the mass as idolatry and the pope as antichrist.

It was not just religious conviction that caused the Scots to rally to Knox's cause. Scottish lords were eager to claim for themselves the church property that had been the pope's. They saw Protestantism as a bulwark of Scottish nationalism against domination of their country by France. Regent Mary of Guise now recognized that toleration was impossible. She gathered a troop of eighteen thousand Scots and Frenchmen to march on Perth, where Knox was preaching, determined to destroy it and Knox. So many Scots rallied to Knox's side, however, that Regent Mary backed down. A few weeks later Knox, still an outlaw, fulfilled his own prophecy and preached again at St. Andrews, where once he had been imprisoned.

An English fleet did help preserve the Scots Protestants from incursion by either Catholic France or Catholic Spain. Queen Elizabeth, however, could never ally her church with that of the author of *The Blast of the Trumpet against the Monstrous Regiment of Women*. Knox wrote her that he had had in mind only the two Catholic Marys. Then, however, with typical lack of tact, he ruined it all by demanding that she humbly repent of her damnable iniquity in having attended mass a few times when Mary had forced her to do so. Elizabeth's Church of England and Knox's Church of Scotland would go separate ways.

With the death of the Regent Mary in 1561, her Catholic daughter, Mary, Queen of Scots, recently widowed in France, assumed the throne in Edinburgh. Young, beautiful, dressed in Paris fashions, she sought to win Knox and the nation by charm rather than force. From his pulpit at St. Giles in Edinburgh Knox denounced the masses being said down the street at the palace and called the queen "a slave of Satan." Mary summoned him to her court repeatedly, argued, pleaded, and wept, to no avail. She then attempted to have Knox condemned as a traitor. He and Protestantism were now too firmly entrenched; Knox was acquitted.

It was Mary's private life that proved her undoing. She had married a Scots lord, Darnley, younger than she. She became so intimate with an Italian court musician and advisor named Riccio, however, that one night her husband and some others broke into the queen's room, where she was dining with Riccio, dragged him out, and murdered him. According to rumor, with Mary's consent Darnley was himself murdered, and Mary promptly married her lover, the man who had murdered Darnley.

It was too much for most Scots. After a battle Mary, Queen of Scots, fled to England. Elizabeth sheltered her, but under a kind of house arrest. When, years later, there was no longer any way to deny that Mary was plotting to overthrow Elizabeth and seize the English throne, Elizabeth ordered Mary beheaded.

By the time of Knox's death Scotland was dominated by Calvinistic Protestantism. In 1560 the Church of Scotland had adopted the Scots Confession, a strongly Calvinistic statement of doctrine largely the work of Knox (still a standard for Presbyterians). They adopted a Book of Discipline, also influenced by Knox. It called not only for a presbyterian form of government of the church but also an ambitious scheme of universal education and of relief of the poor. These were to be supported by one-third of the lands of the church. The greed of Scots nobles, however, prevented its full goal being reached. Knox led in producing the Book of Common Order, closely following the pattern of worship he had seen in Geneva, with more room for free prayers. At his death he left a church determined to resist any effort to reinstitute Catholicism or to be subject to any other nation.

James and Charles

With the end of the reign of Mary, Queen of Scots, her son became King James VI of Scotland, and with the death of Queen Elizabeth he became also King James I of England. At last Scotland and England were united under one ruler. Baptized a Catholic, the son of a Catholic mother, but reared by Protestants in Scotland, James determined to follow the Elizabethan compromise and allow diversity of doctrine but insisted on conformity to the Prayer Book.

James wrote in defense of the divine right of kings:

> *Monarchie* is the trew paterne of Diuinitie . . . Kings are called God by the propheticall King *David.* . . . The duetie, and alleageance of the people to their lawfull king, their obedience, I say, ought to be to him, as to Gods Lieutenant in earth . . . aknowledging him as Iudge set by God ouer them. . . . The King is aboue the law.[8]

James believed, therefore, that "Presbytery agreeth with monarchy as God with the devil"; bishops appointed by the king were essential. Perhaps, he thought, the Scots might agree to have bishops if they did not so much govern as simply collect revenues for the crown. The Scots laughed at such officials as "Tulchan bishops" (stuffed cowskins they used to induce other cows to give milk). James sent the Scots Presbyterian leader Melville into exile and with bribes to Scots lords and the force of the army achieved an acceptable compromise that did give Scottish bishops some authority but left individual congregations relatively free under their elected elders.

James's reign did produce one achievement that was to have great influence on subsequent Protestantism. The official Bible of the Church of England was called "the Bishop's Bible." The most popular Bible of the time, however, was a translation produced in Geneva. It contained notes that were clearly Calvinist. For example, a note on 2 Chronicles 15:16 condemned Asa; when his queen mother worshiped an idol he did remove her from office, but, the note said, he should also have killed her. Remembering the fate of his mother, Mary, Queen of Scots, James did not like those notes. In 1611 a new translation of the Bible was produced, authorized by James, popularly known subsequently as the King James Version. There was strong opposition to this new translation, and for years the Geneva Bible remained more popular, especially with Presbyterians and Puritans. The Book of Common Prayer still makes use of the older version, so that Episcopalians, and the Methodists who derived their liturgy in part from them, continue to pray in the Lord's Prayer that God will forgive them their *trespasses*, while others use the language of the King James translation and pray for forgiveness of their *debts*. More than any other book, the King James version of Scripture has influenced the language and literature of English-speaking people ever since its publication.

Scots Presbyterian resistance to Anglo-Catholic and Roman Catholic liturgy is illustrated in the story of Jenny Geddes. St. Giles, Edinburgh, is probably the only church in the world with a marker commemorating the tradition that there a brave woman in the congregation threw her stool at the minister. Some question whether Jenny Geddes was really the first, but there can be no doubt that it was women who led in a riot there. It came about like this. James I had been willing to compromise, but his son Charles I, whom some believed was at heart a Roman Catholic, was determined to bring the Church of Scotland under his control. He decreed that on July 23, 1637, the service from the Book of Common Prayer would be used in every church. "You'll not say mass in my ear," Jenny Geddes is reported to have shouted, and the rioters drove the priest to flight. Similar riots occurred all over Scotland. Scots were determined to be Presbyterian.

On February 28, 1638, Scots leaders performed what they later called the marriage of their nation to God. At Greyfriars' Church in Edinburgh they signed the National Covenant. For three days ministers, lords, and common people joined in signing that covenant, sometimes in blood. A monument there still honors their heroism. In wars of religion that followed, some eighteen thousand Scots died, but the state Church of Scotland remained Presbyterian.

Since theologically both were Calvinists, in England Presbyterians and Puritans were united for years; together they grew in control of Parliament. By order of Parliament, on July 1, 1643, a distinguished group of mostly English Calvinist theologians met at Westminster Abbey for the first of 1,163 sessions. There they produced the Westminster Confession of Faith and its accompanying catechisms. These would remain the authoritative statement of doctrine for English-speaking Presbyterians and many Congregationalists for more than three hundred years.

So strong was the Puritan-Presbyterian opposition to bishops that Parliament voted to abolish bishops. In retaliation Charles I attempted to have some members of Parliament arrested. The result: Britain entered a period of civil war. On the one hand were the Puritan forces, the "Roundheads," largely from the south, commoners and the merchant class. Siding with the king were the aristocrats, the "Cavaliers." The bloody war ended with the king in the hands of the Scottish army. Charles was beheaded and the Roundheads' general, stern Puritan Oliver Cromwell, ruled, taking the title Lord Protector. For eleven years England was officially Puritan.

Though Presbyterians and English Puritans agreed on theology, once in power it was clear that their difference with regard to church government was serious. Cromwell agreed with Milton that presbyters were simply bishops "writ large," and like bishops they were suppressors of freedom, so he suppressed Presbyterianism. Congregationalism, with each congregation independent and democratic, triumphed. Presbyterianism continued in Scotland but never fully recovered in England.

Cromwell ruled nine years. His son, however, proved a much less capable leader, and the Cavaliers (or Tories) were able to place Charles II, son of Charles I, on the throne. Parliament, however, had gotten used to having the power, and Charles was able to rule only by tolerating his opponents and accepting parliamentary restrictions. He secured a French alliance by promising to make England Catholic, but he never really attempted that transformation. He himself professed Catholicism on his deathbed.

His brother and successor, James II, however, did not hesitate; he began to take steps to move England back into Roman Catholicism. Two months after taking office he put down a Protestant rebellion and executed, tortured, or sent into slavery many Protestant leaders. Many fled to America. His intolerance alienated both parties. After James had ruled three years the Protestants in Parliament invited, from Presbyterian Holland, William of Orange and his wife, Charles's Protestant daughter Mary, to rule in Great Britain. James fled into exile in France.

There continued to be religious strife, and Catholics were still persecuted, but 1688, the year of the "Glorious Revolution" in which William and Mary began their reign, may be thought of as in a sense the end of the Reformation period. People were tiring of religious strife.

Deeper Than the Strife

There were religious wars, and many people were intolerant. There was also, however, deep commitment to Jesus Christ as the various groups understood him. Here is a prayer from this troubled time:

> Keep us, O God, from pettiness; let us be large in thought, in word, in deed.
> Let us be done with faultfinding and leave off self-serving.
> May we put away all pretenses and meet each other, face to face, without
>   self-pity and without prejudice.
> May we never be hasty in judgment and always generous.
> Let us take time for all things; make us to grow calm, serene, gentle.
> Teach us to put in action our better impulses—straightforward and unafraid.
> Grant that we may realize it is the little things of life that create difficulties;
>   that in the big things of life we are as one.
> Oh, Lord, let us not forget to be kind.
> Amen.

The author of that irenic prayer was the devout Christian and Catholic whom Knox called an instrument of Satan, Mary, Queen of Scots.

Thomas Cranmer allowed his belief in the authority of the ruler, now Mary of England, to override his convictions, and, ultimately to his shame, he recanted his Protestant faith. But to Cranmer, more than to any other, is owed the Book of Common Prayer. Its beautiful prayers are beloved by English-speaking Christians far beyond the Episcopal communion. For example:

> Almighty God, to whom all hearts are open,
> all desires known,
> and from whom no secrets are hid:
> Cleanse the thoughts of our hearts
> by the inspiration of your Holy Spirit,
> that we may perfectly love you
> and worthily magnify your holy name;
> through Christ our Lord.
> Amen.

Baptist John Bunyan penned what, next to the Book of Common Prayer, became perhaps the most influential devotional literature written in the period. In his allegory *Pilgrim's Progress* he describes the Christian life as the journey from the City of Destruction to the Heavenly City. At one point Christian and his companion Hopeful are thrown into a dungeon by Giant Despair. All seems lost:

> Now a little before it was day, good Christian, as one half amazed, brake out into this passionate speech: "What a fool," quoth he, "am I to lie in a stinking dungeon, when I may as well walk at liberty! I have a key in my bosom called Promise, that will I am persuaded, open any lock in Doubting Castle."[9]

With the promises of Scripture, Christian is able to escape even Giant Despair. Bunyan knew about prison doors; he wrote those words while in Bedford jail.

Finally, Congregationalists and Presbyterians for more than two hundred years taught their children the Westminster Shorter Catechism. Others who never learned all of it have made their priority in life what it describes in the answer to its first question: Man's chief end is to glorify God, and to enjoy him forever.[10]

Questions Chapter 6

1. If someone said to you, "The Reformation in Great Britain came about because Henry VIII wanted a divorce," how would you reply?

2. Read some prayers from our *Book of Common Worship,* adopted in 1993 by the Cumberland Presbyterian Church and the Presbyterian Church (U.S.A.). About one hundred of its prayers come from the Episcopal *Book of Common Prayer,* originally compiled by the martyr Thomas Cranmer. Which are your favorites?

3. To what extent does the church in our country reflect the ideas of the Puritans? To what extent should it do so?

4. Presbyterianism came to this country largely from the Reformation in Scotland. What did John Knox do to help bring about that Reformation? This chapter's discussion of Knox begins with two contrasting evaluations. What truth, if any, do you find in each?

5. Why would thousands of Scots sign the National Covenant of 1638 and risk their lives for Presbyterianism? Just how important are Presbyterian doctrine and government?

6. In what ways, if any, does your church make use of these great classic statements of Reformed doctrine: the Scots Confession? the Westminster Confession? the Larger and Shorter Catechisms? How might it make better use of them?

Chapter 7

The Church Comes to America (c. 1500–1800)

On October 12, 1492, a devout Italian sailor, carrying the flag of their most Catholic majesties Ferdinand and Isabella of Spain, landed on a little Caribbean island. His first name was "Christopher," meaning "Christ-Bearer." With Columbus the church had come to the New World.

Catholicism Comes to America

In 1776 when the thirteen British colonies declared their independence, Protestantism in its varied forms was far and away their dominant religion. Protestants should remember, however, that to their south and west Spanish and French Catholics had been the first to bring their understanding of the faith to parts of what was to become the United States of America.

Though primarily the Spaniards come for gold from the beginning Spanish incursion into the New World included a missionary purpose. Christopher Columbus's journal reminded Ferdinand and Isabella that they had sent him to the countries of "India" to explore "the proper method of converting them to our holy faith." He had found the natives so friendly, he reported, that he "perceived that they could much more easily be converted to our holy faith by gentle means than by force." No doubt with that purpose still in mind, on his next voyage Columbus brought with him two priests.

The repeated cruelty of the European invaders, Protestant and Catholic, toward the Native Americans is well known. The church did not by any means always remember Columbus's words about using peaceful means for conversion. Critics of early Spanish missionaries have charged that they sometimes baptized groups of "converts" who had not been adequately instructed in the faith. Often the Spaniards tried to enslave them. Less often told, at least among Protestants, is the heroism of those Jesuits, Franciscans, and others who accompanied the Spanish and French adventurers into the new and dangerous world. More than most of the Protestant ministers who came to the thirteen colonies, the Catholic clergy came with the deliberate intention of evangelizing the Native Americans.

The story of those missionaries in Latin America, and the martyrdom they often faced, lies beyond the scope of this book. In Florida, however, missionaries were at work well before the settlements at Jamestown and Plymouth Rock. In 1521, on his second expedition seeking the fountain of youth, Ponce de Leon took with him friars and priests. Early efforts to establish a Spanish colony in Florida were not successful, but the Spanish did not give up. In 1539 Hernando de Soto explored all the way to what was to be called the Mississippi; he named it the "River of the Holy Spirit." Only five of the twelve priests who had started out with him made it back to New Spain. In 1549 Louis Cancer de Barbastro entered Florida as a peaceful missionary without any military protection. He was soon martyred by the "Indians."

In spite of difficulties, on the day of the festival of St. Augustine, 1563, mass was said at what was to become the city of St. Augustine, Florida. A Catholic settlement, the oldest city in what is now the United States, had been formed. The first permanent English settlement, Jamestown, Virginia, was not made until forty-four years later.

Catholics who entered Georgia and South Carolina soon encountered Huguenots; they slaughtered some of them. They boasted that they had done so not because these enemies were French but because they were Protestant. The French Protestants fought back. Often enslaved or slaughtered by the Spaniards, the "Indians" fought back, too. Many brave priests who attempted missions in all these areas were killed.

As early as 1700 French Catholics came down from Canada attempting settlements and missions all along the Mississippi. Louisiana became Catholic territory, and settlements grew up at St. Louis and New Orleans, among others.

Of the thirteen British colonies one, Maryland (Mary's Land), was established as, in part, a refuge for Roman Catholics seeking sanctuary from persecution by their Protestant brothers. In 1625 George Calvert, the first Lord Baltimore and a British secretary of state, converted to Catholicism. He persuaded James I to grant him a charter for a colony, and under his son Cornelius settlement began. From the first it included Protestants as well as Catholics. In 1649 Maryland gained the distinction of being the first colony, and among the first places in the world, where there was enacted an "Act of Toleration Concerning Religion." It decreed that "noe person or persons whatsoever within this Province . . . professing to believe in Jesus Christ, shall from henceforth bee any waies troubled, Molested or discountenanced for or in respect of his of her religion nor in the free exercise thereof."[1] Toleration did not extend to those who denied the Trinity, including Jews; still Catholics had led in taking a remarkable step in the direction of religious freedom.

Protestants would not long tolerate such toleration. Puritans were soon the majority in the colony. When, in 1651, a Catholic replaced Maryland's Puritan governor, Puritans revolted. For a two-year period Protestants made Roman Catholicism illegal even in Catholic Maryland. In 1702 the Church of England, though a relatively small minority, was made the state church. Catholics survived, though as a distrusted minority, barred from office in several colonies. It was not until the early nineteenth century that thousands of Catholic immigrants began to make the Roman Catholic Church the largest religious body in the United States.

The Episcopal Church

Protestantism secured a place in America in 1607. In 1606 James I of England had granted a charter to the Virginia Company that authorized England's first permanent colony in the new world. The charter expressed the hope that the colony "may by the Province of Almighty God, hereafter tend to the Glory of His Divine Majesty, in propagating the Christian Religion to such People as yet live in Darkness and in ignorance of the true Knowledge and Worship of God." When, a year later, the settlers arrived, their first act was to kneel in prayer. They erected a cross, and at Jamestown, Virginia, they planted the first permanent English settlement in America. Their first public building was a wooden and cloth chapel, and soon they erected a stone church. Robert Hunt was approved by the archbishop of Canterbury as the colony's pastor.

From the first the Church of England (the Episcopal Church) was the state church in Virginia, and it was to become the state church in the Carolinas, Georgia, and at times, but less successfully, in other colonies. Virginia's settlers were loyal to the official church; they had not come as did the New England Puritans seeking to reform or escape it. As the state church it reflected the changes that occurred from time to time in the ecclesiastical establishment in England. There was at first a Puritan influence, with laws requiring Sabbath observance and enforcing strict morality. In the reign of Charles II its services tended to be more "high church," with an emphasis on more elaborate liturgy. With the coming of William and Mary, the Church of England, and thus the official church of these colonies, became more Protestant again.

With the backing of the state, the Episcopal Church was the dominant religious force in the southern colonies. At the same time its establishment brought some problems. The first colonists were all church members, but, unlike the Puritans of New England, they did not come for God but for gold. They found that wealth in fertile land, not metal. Few of the first Virginia colonists were dirt farmers; plowing tobacco fields was not something they were used to. They began to "solve" that problem when, twelve years after these white English gentlemen had landed, the first boatload of African slaves arrived at Jamestown to do the manual labor.

The Anglican clergy, supported by the state and endowments, sometimes became like those indolent pastors whose worldliness the Puritans in England protested. Moreover, though they founded the College of William and Mary to educate their ministers, candidates for ordination still had to make the long and expensive trip to London for ordination by a bishop. Just as the English wanted to keep secular government in the mother country, so they were hesitant to send bishops to the distant colonies. The church soon faced a shortage of pastors. The parish system of the church in relatively densely populated England did not work as well in Virginia, where the settlers were often scattered in their large plantations.

One who was determined to overcome obstacles and help the Church of England perform its mission in the New World was an English clergyman named Thomas Bray, commissioned to go to Maryland to see what improvements could be made there. What he found, he said, was "gross ignorance of the principles of the Christian religion." Though he was in the colonies only ten weeks, when he returned to England he gave leadership to several projects that gave life to the colonial church. One of these was the Society for the Promotion of Christian Knowledge. It established some thirty-nine libraries in the colonies and many more in England. It continues its educational ministry today, publishing and distributing Christian literature. He also led in the establishment of the Society for the Propagation of the Gospel in Foreign Parts, which in 1701 began a program that was to sponsor some three hundred missionaries to the colonies over the next century. Bray also worked for ministry to slaves, for the establishment of hospitals, and for prison reform. When in 1733 James Oglethorpe founded the colony of Georgia, planned for the relief of debtors, he owed his idea, in part, to Bray.

Nevertheless, the Anglican Church continued to be dependent upon bishops on the other side of the Atlantic and on state and endowment support. Deism considerably influenced the theology of its ministers, and Deism was not a belief that produced evangelistic zeal. The Anglican Church began to lose people, especially in the west and among the poor, to Presbyterians, Methodists, and Baptists, who seemed able to capitalize better on a new eighteenth-century revival movement called the "Great Awakening."

The Plymouth Pilgrims

Soon after the Episcopalians arrived in Virginia, some spiritual ancestors of what, centuries later, came to be called the United Church of Christ began arriving in New England.

Scrooby—the name of this English village is not familiar to most Americans. The story of the little congregation that once called Scrooby home, however, was to become part of the legend and even a mythology loved by American Protestantism for four hundred years.

About 1575 William Brewster became bailiff of Scrooby Manor. Each Sabbath he and his son William heard the pastor at nearby Balworth, Richard Clayton, preaching the new Puritan doctrines of John Calvin. There Brewster met a twelve-year-old farm youth, William Bradford, who became like a son to him. Bradford would one day be governor of the Plymouth Plantation.

Brewster sent his own son, William III, to Cambridge. There he was in school with six young men who, subsequently, would be martyred for their adherence to their Puritan faith. Upon graduation young William served as a diplomat in Holland and held a position in the court in London. Soon, however, he returned to Scrooby, where he inherited his father's position. There a group of Separatists had begun meeting in Scrooby Manor, with John Robinson as their pastor. At one point the congregation numbered about 150. Gradually it became clear, however, that they could not remain in England. On September 7, 1607, William Brewster resigned his position as postmaster, perhaps being forced to do so because of his beliefs. Two months later he was ordered to appear in court, charged with "disobedience in matters of religion." He failed to appear, and the police could not find him. One dark night the whole congregation boarded a ship bound for Presbyterian Holland, where they could freely practice their religion. They were victims of a cruel joke. As soon as they were all on board, the crew seized them, searched through their baggage and even the clothes they were wearing, both men and women, stole everything valuable, and hauled them off to jail. After about a month, however, all but seven were released; the authorities did not know quite what to do with all these women and children.

They tried again. This time the men went on board first to make sure there was no trickery. Suddenly they heard in the distance the sounds of an armed mob coming to attack them. Panicked, the Dutch sailors put to sea, leaving the women and children on the shore.

Eventually the group was reunited in Amsterdam and settled down in Leyden, in Presbyterian Holland. As to theology, they got along well with the Dutch Calvinists. Brewster became a lecturer at Leyden University, where he defended the double-election, predestination doctrines of Calvin against the

Arminian "heresy." The Dutch, however, even though Calvinists, were too worldly for these strict Separatists. Moreover, the Pilgrims were loyal English men and women, speaking English, not Dutch, and were never quite at home in Holland.

They did sometimes share Communion with a Presbyterian congregation from England. It was that connection, in part, that made trouble for their elder, Brewster. Like other English Calvinists, he loved to write and print pamphlets, and some of his writings defending the Presbyterian position aroused the ire of King James of England. He undertook to arrest Brewster in Leyden. The police found he had gone to Amsterdam. They arrived there too late; he was back in England. When they sought him at Southampton they discovered that he had slipped back into Holland. They settled for throwing his assistant in jail.

It was time to go. There were economic and other cultural factors, but William Bradford wrote of the big reason: "a great hope and inward zeal they had of laying some good foundation, or at least to make some way there unto for the propagating and advancing the gospel of the kingdom of Christ in those remote parts of the world, yet though they should be but even as stepping stones with others for the performing of so great a work."[2]

They were not the first Separatist refugees to flee to Holland and then attempt a colony in America. Under Francis Johnson two hundred had packed into a little boat and headed for the New World. Disease broke out. When the ship finally landed at Chesapeake Bay, of that two hundred only fifty were still alive. They soon scattered, unable to form a permanent settlement.

The Pilgrims were devastated by news of that disaster. They realized that only the youngest and strongest should attempt the voyage. They spent a day in fasting, and Pastor Robinson, knowing that he was too old to go, preached a farewell sermon. Be open in the New World to new ideas, he said. "God has yet more light to break forth from his holy word."

An unscrupulous entrepreneur named Thomas Weston provided them two ships but squeezed them for every penny they had. Even then one boat, the *Speedwell*, proved unseaworthy. Finally 102 passengers and crew loaded onto the *Mayflower* and set out. Thirty-two were children, and at least two of the women were pregnant. One child was born on the voyage, named, appropriately, Oceanus; another was born as they anchored off New England.

The night before they debarked they signed the "The Mayflower Compact." It declared that "Having undertaken for ye glorie of God, and advancement of ye Christian faith and honour of our king & countrie," they now undertook to form a covenant for "just and equall Lawes." It was November 11, 1620.

Now entries in their journal begin to read like this: "December 21—This day died Solomon Nathan, the sixth to die this month. . . . Jan. 29—dies Rose, wife of Captain Standish. N.B. this month 9 of our number die. . . . Feb. 21, died Mr. William White. . . . This month 17 of our number die."

Nevertheless half of the Pilgrims survived the winter. Aided by friendly Native Americans they planted crops and harvested fish. And with their new "Indian" friends, the next fall they feasted. That thanksgiving inspired the legend celebrated in America's only unique religious holiday.

The Puritan Dream

The Plymouth colony was eventually absorbed into the commonwealth of the thousands of Puritans who soon began settling New England. The goal of the Puritan leaders was to establish a colony not only for the kingdom of Great Britain but also for the kingdom of God.

The first great leader of this remarkable group was John Winthrop. In 1630, on board the *Arabella,* one of the ships that brought the first Puritans to New England, he wrote:

> wee must delight in eache other, make others Condicions our owne, rejoyce together, mourne together labour, and suffer together . . . that men shall say of succeeding plantacious: the lord make it like that of New England: for we must Consider that wee shall be as a Citty upon a Hill, the eies of all people are uppon us. . . . But if our heartes shall turne away . . . wee shall surely perishe out of the good Land whether wee passe over this vast Sea to possesse it.[3]

Winthrop was wise to call upon his followers to be willing to suffer together; of the first thousand who made the trip two hundred soon returned to England, and two hundred others died the first winter. Yet in the next ten years some twenty thousand had come to the colony.

They had come with an apocalyptic vision. If they remained faithful, in New England God might bring at last the new Jerusalem in a new earth. United in faith and practice, they would be a colony of God's kingdom, an ideal community.

They worshiped. Perhaps if you had joined them on a Sunday morning you might have shared in a service like the one described by a Puritan back in England:

> This day was one of the sweetest I have seen. . . . After Dr. Twisee had begun with a briefe prayer, Mr. Marshall prayed large two houres, most divinelie, confessing the sins of the members of the Assemblie in a wonderful pathetick, and prudent way. After, Mr. Arrowsmith preached one houre, then a psalm; thereafter, Mr. Vines prayed near two houres.[4]

More often, however, you would hear a sermon that lasted two or three hours, with only an hour or so devoted to prayer. You and your spouse would be on opposite sides of the simple meeting house. The Scripture would be read from the Geneva Bible—still preferred to the King James Version—and the song would be a psalm, not a hymn. There would be no "kit o' whistles" (organ), and one reporter admits that the singing was usually not very good. You would return for further instruction in the afternoon. The doctrines of Calvinism would be preached. Each weekday the husband would lead all the family in prayer.

Responsible historians refute the charge that Puritans were people terrified by the thought of enjoying themselves and given to burning witches. They simply tried to make sure that worldly amusements did not crowd out devotion to God. They liked to eat well, and they all drank, though moderately. Their dress, though simple, was not always drab and might include a red vest. They loved sports. And the love letters Governor Winthrop wrote his wife, when for a year they were separated by an ocean, bear moving witness to the fact that romantic, married love was part of Puritan life.

They tried to preserve their model community by prayers, sermons, and self-examination. They also enacted laws to protect the faith. Soon, however, there were Quakers and others who preached what seemed heretical doctrines. For example, "heretic" Mary Dyer was expelled from the colony. In 1660 she returned as a Quaker missionary. Arrested, she was forced to watch her associates hanged. Blindfolded, she herself was led to the gallows. Perhaps having regard to her sex, the Puritan fathers then let her go. But when she returned to preach again she was executed as an enemy of true religion.

Gradually these Puritans became Separatists. Indeed, fear of Episcopal establishment was one of the many factors that brought agitation for America's independence in New England. In 1769 an imaginative political cartoon pictured an English boat bringing an Episcopal bishop. As it attempted to land it was being pushed back into the sea, while New England Puritans threw at it books by philosopher John Locke and theologian John Calvin.

A worse threat to the Puritan dream was that succeeding generations, grown prosperous by Puritan industriousness, began to become worldly and indifferent to religion of any kind.

The First Great Awakening

At times there were revivals. Familiar with the sedate worship traditional among Puritans, had you worshiped in Northampton, Massachusetts, in the 1730s, you might have been shocked. You might have seen someone fainting and heard people openly weeping or crying out with terror because of their sins, or laughing with joy because of their salvation. You would have seen people, especially young people, gathering in groups later to discuss with the pastor, or simply with one another, the truths of the sermon. The preacher, Jonathan Edwards, had no desire for sensationalism; he read his scholarly sermons. He measured the revival not in terms of the tears or shouts but in the renewed interest in religion and in changed lives. For no human reason this Calvinist could think of but simply because of what he called a "Surprising Work of God," they were experiencing a revival soon spoken of as the "Great Awakening."

Edwards had served as the pastor of a Presbyterian church in New York and as a teacher at Yale. He ended his career as president of the College of New Jersey (later Princeton), founded in part because of Presbyterian influence. He is still recognized as one of the outstanding theologians in American history. Though his most famous sermon is "Sinners in the Hands of an Angry God," his typical message was Calvin's sovereign love of God saving hell-deserving sinners. Even one's choice to be a Christian is a pure gift of the Holy Spirit, God's election, not ours, he argued. Bound by sin, by nature a human has no free will to choose to believe; only grace saves.

The Great Awakening spread through New England. The eloquent preacher George Whitefield helped spread it elsewhere. In England he had been a friend of John Wesley, founder of Methodism, but he never actually became a Methodist. "Father Abraham," Whitefield declaimed, "whom have you in heaven? Any Episcopalians? No! Any Presbyterians? No! Any Independents or Methodists? No! No! No! We don't know those names here. All who are here are Christians." He too was a Calvinist, preaching God's sovereign, irresistible grace. Throughout the south and on up through the middle colonies into New England thousands flocked to hear Whitefield. Benjamin Franklin was sufficiently impressed to contribute money. He remained unconverted. however; he wrote that though Whitefield prayed for him those prayers were never answered. Thousands of others did profess conversion, and many churches were strengthened.

The Baptists

Not all church leaders approved of the Great Awakening. The Episcopal Church, lacking ministers and wedded to formal services using the Book of Common Prayer, was never able to profit by the revival as much as some other groups. Moreover, clergy of the established church seemed indolent and worldly to those fired by the Great Awakening. Among those whose numbers multiplied with the new movement were the Baptists, even though they faced persecution.

Determined to preserve the purity of the faith for which they had established their colony, the Puritans banished Roger Williams from Massachusetts. He had preached the separation of church and state. He became, at least for a while, a Baptist. In 1636 he founded the colony of Rhode Island, with its guarantee of religious liberty. Baptists rightly glory in the fact that they have pioneered in crusading for religious freedom and boast that they have never persecuted anyone.

John Clarke, pastor of the Newport Baptist Church beginning some time around 1640, has been called the father of Baptists in America. Police entered his home to arrest him for preaching Baptist doctrines.

Henry Dunster, the first president of Harvard, was forced to resign. There was no question of his scholarship or his religious commitment. What disqualified him in the eyes of the New England Congregationalists was that he had become a Baptist. He pleaded that his wife and family be allowed to occupy the president's home at least through the rest of the cold Massachusetts winter. The authorities in Congregationalist Massachusetts refused.

One factor in Dunster's resolve to be a Baptist was the witness of Obadiah Holmes. Arrested for his stand as a Baptist, Holmes refused to accept the fine offered by a friend. Instead he accepted a brutal beating.

Especially in the south Baptists profited by the Great Awakening, in spite of persecution. In 1763 Col. Samuel Harriss, a Baptist, was mobbed and beaten with sticks, whips, and clubs in Culpepper County, Virginia. In Orange County a mob dragged this Baptist down the street by his hair. In Virginia an Episcopal parson led the mob that attacked and beat Baptist John Walter. Between 1765 and 1776 thirty-four Virginia Baptists were imprisoned. The excuse given was that Baptists were cruel to children in denying them baptism.

Despite persecution the Baptists grew with amazing rapidity, especially among the unsophisticated rural frontiersmen. To start a Baptist church you did not have to send a man to England for ordination, as did the Episcopalians, or send him east for advanced education, as did the Presbyterians. You did not even have to wait for the monthly visit of the Methodist circuit rider. Most Baptist ministers were farmers, living off the land while serving churches. Better than others, Baptists seemed to speak the language of their hearers. Rejecting infant baptism, they called for repentance and conversion as adults as a requirement for membership. Baptism by immersion dramatized that conversion. Their gospel, affirming God's grace but calling sinners to personal decision and rebirth, stirred the hearts of thousands.

The Methodists

Methodists too were at home in the Great Awakening. In England John Wesley, founder of Methodism, had preached to thousands, not only in churches but in fields and at the entrances to mines. When bishops of the Church of England, of which he was a loyal priest, attempted to restrain him to a single area, he is said to have replied, "All the world is my parish." On foot or on horseback he traveled the equivalent of ten times around the world. He is said to have preached fifty thousand sermons, while his brother Charles wrote sixty-five hundred hymns. (Many of Charles Wesley's hymns have been sung by Christians of many denominations ever since.) The effect of the Methodist revival on the laboring people of England is said to have been so profound that it was reflected in the improved quality of English cloth. Used to revival preaching, the Methodists were able to join effectively in America's revival.

Moravians had a share in Wesley's change from being a "high church" Episcopalian. On a voyage to a not very successful pastorate in Georgia, Wesley had been impressed by the Moravians' piety and courage at sea. Back in England in 1735, Moravians counseled with him, reassuring him of salvation by grace. Thus influenced, at a small group meeting in Aldersgate he "felt his heart strangely warmed." Mission-minded, like the Moravians, he began to preach everywhere. In 1769 the Methodists sent two missionaries from England to New York: Richard Boardman and Joseph Pilmoor. The Methodists' first annual conference was convened in Philadelphia in 1773.

Wesley had already rejected the Church of England's emphasis on apostolic succession. In 1784 he himself began to ordain ministers. The Methodist theology departed from strict Calvinism by affirming that while salvation is indeed by grace alone, individuals have free will to accept or reject that salvation. The emphasis in Methodist societies, however, was not on uniformity of belief but on godly living. Members were asked to examine themselves and to help one another as disciples. Soon ministers were expected to follow a book of discipline that, among many rules, required strict observance of the Sabbath and forbade smoking.

Among those ordained and soon to be successfully spreading the gospel in America were Thomas Coke and Francis Asbury. One monument to their ministry is the churches they helped found; another is that their names are remembered in the combination "Cokesbury." For many years Cokesbury bookstores and literature have enriched the faith of Christians in many denominations.

A loyal Englishman, Wesley strongly opposed the American Revolution. That unpopular stand temporarily slowed the Methodist advance, but Methodists continued to spread their gospel. The typical Methodist preacher was a

circuit rider, going on horseback from place to place among the farms and frontier settlements. Especially in the south, this system helped Methodists reach
the pioneers more effectively than any other group except the Baptists.

Quakers, Lutherans, and Moravians

Perhaps not quite seriously, some Quakers are said to pray, "Lord, makes us
as good as the rest of the world thinks we are." Down through the years
the Quakers have indeed earned the reputation of being, as their proper name
calls them, the "Society of Friends." These Friends have been quiet workers
for peace and justice throughout their history, with influence far beyond their
numbers.

Their founder, George Fox, proposed that anyone today may be open to the
Inner Light even as were those who wrote books of the Bible. The Spirit in
each heart rather than the Scriptures should be our guide. At first not so quiet,
Fox proclaimed his message not only in public places but in churches and was
repeatedly arrested not only for heresy but for disturbing public worship. His
followers, however, soon formed orderly and peaceful fellowships.

Among those who were imprisoned was a young convert named William
Penn. Having good family connections, he was able to persuade Charles II to
grant him a charter, and Penn's Woods would eventually become the state of
Pennsylvania. In the peaceful Quaker fashion he made a treaty of friendship
with the Native Americans, and he opened the colony, which he called a "Holy
Experiment," to all denominations. The chief city was named Philadelphia,
meaning the "city of brotherly love." Pennsylvania became a refuge for many
kinds of Christians. Reared in Congregationalist New England, John Adams
was impressed by the variety he found in the Quaker city. When in Philadelphia for the convention that would adopt the Declaration of Independence, on
Sundays he would often attend three services. With appreciation he could and
did sample Anglican, Methodist, Baptist, Presbyterian, Moravian, and Roman
Catholic worship, as well as that of the Quakers.

Quaker settlement grew, and the Friends were a major American denomination in the eighteenth century. In part because of their unpopular stands
against slavery and against war, later they declined in numbers.

Establishing settlements with biblical names like Bethlehem and Salem—
now Winston Salem—were the Moravians. With ties going back even before
the Reformation to John Hus, these Pietists became in a sense the missionary
arm of German Protestantism. Far beyond their numbers in this country, they
influenced many others, including John Wesley, and they have continued to

carry on a ministry of evangelism, peace, and good works in distant and difficult places around the world.

In 1619 Rasmus Jensen conducted a Lutheran service beside Hudson Bay, and in 1638 in Wilmington, Delaware, the first Lutheran church in America was erected. The first book translated into a Native American dialect was Luther's Small Catechism. By 1800 Lutherans made up perhaps nine percent of the American population. The great growth of Lutheranism in America was to come later, however, with the nineteenth century's mass immigration from Germany and Scandinavia. But a foundation had been laid to receive them, especially by "the Patriarch of the Lutheran Church in America," Henry Melchior Muhlenberg. He arrived in 1743 and was soon announcing, "The church must be planted!" To achieve that goal he traveled from colony to colony, organizing churches and bringing strength to Lutheranism.

In 1775 Muhlenberg's son, John, a pastor in Woodstock, Virginia, led the morning worship, preached his sermon, and then pulled open his ministerial robe. Beneath it he was dressed in the uniform of the Continental army. The American Revolution was at hand.

The Faith of the Founders

While the well-known founders put in writing the great documents of American independence, it was to a considerable extent now forgotten Protestant clergy, especially the Congregationalists, Baptists, and Presbyterians, who stirred up the people to demand independence. It is interesting, however, to look at the religious beliefs of the founders.

Some have argued that the religion of most of the designers of America's Declaration of Independence and Constitution were at best Deists, and that their basic motivation was not religious but wholly secular. By contrast, historian Richard Hofstadter argues, "The men who drew up the Constitution in 1787 had a vivid Calvinistic sense of human evil and damnation and believed with Hobbes that men are selfish and contentious."[5] That view was not Deistic. More recently Michael Novak has argued that the founders' motivation was a combination of "humble faith and common sense."[6] Among signers of the Declaration of Independence, John Witherspoon, Benjamin Rush, and some others were orthodox Calvinists, but most were not. In a sense most of them were Deists, yet few if any were skeptical Deists like Thomas Paine. Deism grew up as a reaction to the religious wars that had torn Europe for centuries. It argued that the essentials are simply the beliefs, which it considered rational, in a Creator, in ethical living, and, perhaps, in a future life. Paine roundly damned all churches and set out to show that the Bible is a book of absurdities and contradictions. Even Benjamin Franklin, who called himself a Deist, was shocked an Paine's negativism and his rejection of the concept of a Providence that might intervene for justice in human affairs. Rigid Deists believed that God always acted according to set laws, but many of the founders prayed for God to come to the aid of the American troops and thanked God when victory was won. One could at least claim to be an orthodox Christian and hold some basic propositions of Deism.[7]

Most of the founders were at least nominally members of churches. Washington was a vestryman in the Anglican church near his home, and its records list his occasional participation in seeing that certain repairs were made and money raised. Jefferson reacted against the Anglican clergy he encountered as a youth, but, calling himself "a *real* Christian," he produced his own "rational" version of the New Testament, with all miracles, including the resurrection, left out. James Madison, like Jefferson, was repelled by the established clergy in Virginia and was never active in the church. He learned his political philosophy, however, from Scottish Presbyterian John Witherspoon, president of the College of New Jersey (Princeton) and his beloved mentor.[8]

From the faith of these and other founders Americans inherited at least three things: (1) They gave America a republican system of government that, as John Adams put it, was the political application of the Golden Rule. The Calvinistic element, urged especially by Adams, was the distrust of human nature, embodied in a system of checks and balances that realistically set limits on rule by the majority of the moment and on the lust of sinful, power-hungry individuals. (2) They argued forcefully that the maintenance of the nation to which they had given birth depended on morality, and morality depended on religion. (3) With the first amendment they attempted to guarantee that Congress would "make no law respecting an establishment of religion, or prohibiting the free exercise thereof." As Jefferson wrote in a reply to a letter from the Baptist congregation in Danbury, Connecticut, they had attempted to end persecution and erect a "wall of separation" between church and state.

Francis Makemie

One who helped to bring about the freedom of religion was the pioneer Presbyterian missionary Francis Makemie. Since chapter nine of this book is devoted to the history of the Presbyterian Church in this country, this chapter has not described the spread of Presbyterianism in the colonies. But it would be incomplete it if did not at least mention Makemie.

He had come from Ireland in 1681 commissioned by an Irish presbytery to be a missionary. They sent him in response to a plea by some Maryland laymen.

Supporting himself as a merchant, Makemie preached up and down the coast, founding Presbyterian churches on the eastern shore of Virginia, in Maryland, and in New York. That colony was officially Anglican, and Governor Cornbury intended to keep it that way. When Makemie preached, even though it was in a home, he was arrested. He spent six weeks in jail.

"He is a Preacher, a Doctor of Physick, a Merchant, and Attorney, or Counsellor at Law, and which is worst of all, a Disturber of Governments"—so charged his judge, Lord Cornbury, when Makemie was put on trial. "How dare you take upon you to Preach in my Government without my License?" Cornbury demanded.

Makemie knew the law, and he cited various statutes that in fact guaranteed him the right to preach. More importantly, he declaimed, "If his Lordship required it, we would give Security for our Behaviour, but to give Bond and Security to Preach no more in your Excellency's Government, if invited and desired by any people, we neither can, nor dare do."

"Then you must go to Gaol."

"We are neither ashamed nor afraid of what we have done," the Presbyterian missionary replied. His stand drew support from all over the colonies.

At length Makemie won his liberty, and Cornbury was recalled to London in disgrace. Cornbury did make Makemie pay the court costs, a year's salary for a Presbyterian minister. Makemie went on to preach on such texts as "We ought to obey God rather than men."

Presbyterian Makemie was ahead of his time in taking a stand for liberty that brought conflict with British authority. By the 1770s many ministers thundered that the sinful colonies had allowed themselves to fall under the domination of a tyrant and that God's judgment would fall upon them if they did not repent. The way of repentance was to throw off that tyranny. And, thus aroused, they did!

Freed from British domination, by 1800 the American church found itself a collection of many different denominations, sometimes competing with one another. Though there was still not complete freedom of religion, America was moving that way and toward yet another revival.

Some Early American Christians

Here are three glimpses of early American faith. The first American poet was Anne Bradstreet. She had sailed for New England on the *Arabella* with

John Winthrop and the first Puritan settlers. During the next forty years she bore her beloved husband eight children, survived ill health and hardships, helped build and maintain a home in the wilderness, and wrote poems such as the following:

> By night when others soundly slept,
> And had at once both ease and rest,
> My waking eyes were open kept
> And so to lie I found it best.
>
> I sought Him whom my soul did love,
> With tears I sought Him earnestly.
> He bowed His ear down from above.
> In vain I did not seek or cry.
>
> My hungry soul He filled with good,
> He in His bottle put my tears,
> My smarting wounds washed in His blood,
> And banished thence my doubts and fears.
>
> What to my Savior shall I give,
> Who freely hath done this for me?
> I'll serve Him here whilst I shall live
> And love Him to eternity.

John Woolman traveled extensively in the colonies in the mid-eighteenth century, visiting Quaker homes and meetings. This excerpt from his journal describes an "edifying" Friends meeting:

> Near the conclusion of the meeting for business, Friends were incited to constancy in supporting the testimony of truth, and reminded of the necessity which the disciples of Christ are under to attend principally to His business as He is pleased to open it to us, and to be particularly careful to have our minds redeemed from the love of wealth, and our outward affairs in as little room as may be, that no temporal concerns may entangle our affections, or hinder us from diligently following the dictates of truth in labouring to promote the pure spirit of meekness and heavenly-mindedness amongst the children of men in these days of calamity and distress, wherein God is visiting our land with His just judgments.

Finally, well into the twentieth century school children were expected to be familiar with George Washington's Farewell Address, including a statement typical of America's founders:

Of all dispositions and habits which lead to political prosperity, religion and morality are indispensable supports. In vain would that man claim the tribute of patriotism who should labor to subvert these great pillars of human happiness—the first props of the duties of man and citizens. The mere politician, equally with the pious man, ought to respect and to cherish them. A volume would not trace all these connections with private and public felicity. . . . Reason and experience both forbid us to expect that national morality can prevail to the exclusion of religious principles.

From time to time America would test the validity of its first president's words.

Questions Chapter 7

1. Why, do you suppose, was the church the first building the settlers erected in the first permanent English-speaking settlement in the New World? What does that fact teach us?
2. In what ways does the story of the Pilgrims and their Plymouth Colony serve as a symbol of the best in American history?
3. What do you think of the Puritans' dream of making America the kingdom of God?
4. What can Presbyterians learn from Baptist history and from Baptists today? from Methodists? from other denominations' histories and practices today? To what extent does it seem to you that the differences in Protestant denominations today are matters of historical origins, and to what extent are they differences of current doctrine and practice?
5. How relevant today are the words quoted from George Washington's Farewell Address? What should we do about the hopes and concerns for America he and other founders expressed?
6. For what truths was Presbyterian pioneer missionary Francis Makemie willing to risk his life? How are those principles challenged today?

Chapter 8

American Churches in
Recent Centuries (c. 1800–Present)

*T*he freedom of religion so dear to the heart of most of America's founders was not fully attained with the adoption of the Constitution. Though the First Amendment to that document guaranteed that as far as the federal government was concerned there would be no law "respecting an establishment of religion or prohibiting the free exercise thereof," several states were slow to establish similar laws. Not until 1826 did Maryland allow Jews to vote, and until the 1830s Congregationalists were still the state church in Massachusetts. In 1886 North Carolina finally made it legal for people who were not Christians to hold public office. When in 1843 Jews in New York protested one public school text-book, the investigating committee found no merit in their complaint. The book, they said, simply taught the principles of Christianity; who could object to that!

Nevertheless, there was such freedom of religion in the new country that soon it was filled with adherents of every variety of Christianity; and indeed people of other faiths began to find homes in the New World. Not always, however, did Protestants welcome Catholics.

Roman Catholics and the Orthodox

By the middle of the nineteenth century some right-wing Protestants were panicked. As they saw it, a horde of foreigners, pledged to absolute obedience to a foreign prelate, were invading the land that had been established to be the Protestant version of the kingdom of God.

At the time of the Revolution, Roman Catholics had made up a tiny minority of the population. As the twenty-first century began, Catholics were far and away America's largest denomination. The 1845 blight on the potato crop in Ireland sparked the immigration of hundreds of thousands of Catholics to this country, loyal to their religion. German Catholic immigration mushroomed too. An average of 140,000 immigrants yearly arrived in the 1840s. With the influx of thousands of Italians, in the first decade of the 1900s the number grew until more than 800,000 Catholics were coming each year. In 1924 Congress passed immigration laws to slow down what seemed to some Protestants an overwhelming invasion.

As early as 1835 a Boston mob, incited by a false rumor that young girls were being imprisoned there, burned an Ursuline convent. Riding a tide of anti-Catholicism, the American (or "Know Nothing") Party elected seventy-five men to the United States Congress. The next year Know Nothings halted erection of the Washington Monument; they had learned that the pope had donated one of its marble stones.

The work of the Roman Catholic Church to welcome these immigrants has been truly remarkable. Earlier, bishops John Carroll and John England had laid a foundation. Elizabeth Ann Seton, a Catholic convert, had opened one of the first Catholic educational institutions, a school for girls, and in 1809 she founded the Sisters of Charity. "Mother Seton" became the first American to be declared a saint. Now, as the immigrants began to pour in, the church not only built congregations but helped shelter the often penniless newcomers, find them jobs, build excellent parochial schools and universities, and establish hospitals all over the United States.

In 1794 the first Russian Orthodox churches in the new world were established in Alaska, which at that time belonged to Russia. The immigration of 1890–1920 brought to American hundreds of thousands from Poland, Russia, Greece, the Slavic countries, and as far east as Syria, with their varied cultures and forms of Orthodoxy. They faced the same problems of prejudice and integration that the Roman Catholics were confronting. One blow to the Russian Orthodox church here was that its state support from Russia ended with the Russian revolution. Greek Orthodox immigrants in America were still divided by conflicts occurring in southeast Europe. One development that helped to bring considerable unity to Orthodoxy and to make it more at home in America's democratic culture was the institution of clergy-lay convocations, unheard of in European Orthodox churches. The Orthodox churches in America claim some two million members and they are reaching out to people beyond their original ethnic roots.

Revivals and the Second Great Awakening

Among Protestants, by contrast, religion seemed at low ebb. In 1798 the newly organized Presbyterian General Assembly, moderated by John Witherspoon, received a gloomy report. "The eternal God," it lamented, "has a controversy with this nation." Other denominations agreed. One estimate is that at that time only one in ten Americans was a church member. The reason was not entirely lack of faith. Some people felt excluded by the high standards for membership in some churches. Some could not find what they regarded as the correct denomination in their communities. And ministers were scarce on the frontier. But it was also true that many preachers felt that in the new nation religion itself was in a serious decline. At the College of New Jersey (later Princeton University), where Witherspoon was president and which had been established with Presbyterian support, only three students were professing Christians.

That was about to change. In 1801 in Cane Ridge, Kentucky, strange things started happening. Thousands of frontier people had gathered to hear the gospel. One observer reports "impassioned exhortations; earnest prayers, sobs, shrieks, or shouts . . . sudden spasms," barking like dogs, and "the jerks," in which, under conviction, converts' bodies twitched and writhed. Not only men but women preached. Thousands professed conversion. The Second Great Awakening was under way.

Though the camp meeting in Kentucky did include emotional outbursts, the Second Great Awakening was by no means confined to that kind of religion. Out of it many were won to faith, strengthening old denominations, and several new denominations were born. Alexander Campbell, aware that the converts had come from many backgrounds, resolved to reconstruct the church on New Testament principles, with no denominations. His followers would simply be "Christians." The Christian Church (Disciples of Christ) emerged through his leadership, and the Churches of Christ also grew out of this movement. As will be noted in the next chapter, some Presbyterians, newly awakened to evangelistic zeal, formed the Cumberland Presbyterian Church.

It was the Methodists and the Baptists, however, who profited most from the new movement. On horseback Methodist circuit riders rode from place to place throughout the frontier, preaching, as had Wesley, indoors or outdoors, wherever there was opportunity. Baptist farmers felt the call and served as pastors for churches in their communities. Jonathan Edwards, a leading figure in the First Great Awakening, had been a "high" Calvinist, arguing that a sinful human could never decide to become a Christian except though God's decision of predestined grace. Perhaps the theology of Baptists and Methodists seemed better related to revivals; revival preachers challenged the sinful hearers to make their own decisions for Christ. Episcopalians and many Presbyterians never felt at ease with the emotionalism of the revivals and the informality of their worship.

It was his emphasis on decision rather than election that led perhaps the greatest evangelist of the mid-nineteenth century, Charles G. Finney, to leave the Presbyterian Church. Earlier evangelists had urged their hearers to make use of "the means of grace" (Bible study and prayer) in hope of receiving assurance of their election. Instead Finney argued that "faith is an act of the will," and he called for immediate decision then and there. God does not want sinners to continue on the road to hell, he pleaded. "God pities and deeply yearns over you," Finney promised sinners. "Go pour out your tears, your prayer, your confessions, your souls before him." Thousands did so. Finney developed techniques for setting up and conducting what came to be called "protracted meetings." An opponent charged that "the practice of females praying in promiscuous [mixed] assemblies is considered absolutely indispensable." Indeed, women were often among those moved to pray out loud at revival meetings. Many times it was women who prepared for the revival by holding prayer meetings in homes. Finney learned how to use emotion-building hymns to open hearts. He would invite those being converted to come to "the anxious bench" to weep and pray. After the service there would be an inquiry meeting. Later evangelists such as Dwight L. Moody, Billy Sunday, and Billy Graham were to follow in his footsteps, perfecting Finney's techniques. Well into the twentieth century many congregations, especially in the south, continued to look to an annual revival meeting as an important element in their program of evangelism, and evangelism was regarded as basic to their mission. Many congregations made a closing invitation to come forward and "take Christ as savior" a regular part of their Sunday morning worship.

The Baptists were deeply committed to this kind of evangelism, and they were so successful in reaching the masses that they grew more rapidly than any other denomination. Their growth continued, and by the middle of the twentieth century Baptists had become by far the largest Protestant denomination. The Methodists became second largest, and that has continued into the twenty-first century.

The World Mission Movement

The nineteenth century's great emphasis on reaching people who were not Christians was relatively new among Protestants. Other than Jews, European Christians had scarcely encountered people who were not professing Christians. Confronted with the Native Americans, they were uncertain whether to kill them or convert them. From early times, however, there were missionaries who attempted to spread the gospel among the "Indians," to build schools, and to help them adjust to the new civilization that began to surround them. When in 1838 Congress forced the Cherokee nation to leave Carolina and take what is now called "the Trail of Tears" to Oklahoma, some four thousand died on their march. Missionary Elizur Butler shared their hardships. Missions to the Native Americans helped inspire American Christians of the nineteenth century to join with their European sisters and brothers to send missionaries all over the world.

In the middle of the twentieth century historian Kenneth Scott Latourette wrote a massive seven-volume *History of the Expansion of Christianity.* So great was the spread of the gospel in the nineteenth century that he devoted three of his seven volumes to just the years 1815 to 1915. "Never before in a period of equal length had Christianity or any other religion penetrated for the first time as large an area as it had in the nineteenth century." "Never before had so many hundreds of thousands contributed voluntarily of their means to assist the spread of the Christianity or any other religion." The nineteenth was, he said, "the great century." Mission activity was by no means confined to Protestants or to Americans, but American Protestants did their share and more.

The modern Protestant missionary movement is often said to begin with William Carey. An English shoe cobbler and Baptist preacher, in the early 1800s his writings began to inspire others to follow him in missionary activity. He spent forty years in India, preaching, translating the Bible, building schools, fighting slavery, and protesting the sacrificing of infants and the burning of widows on the funeral piles of their husbands.

The American part of the movement for overseas missions is sometimes said to have begun in a haystack. It was in 1806 in an outdoor prayer meeting, moved for shelter under a haystack when a storm began, that five Williams College students began to feel a new call to spread the gospel to "the heathen." They spread this concern, and in 1812 American Adoniram Judson and his wife Ann began work in Burma. They labored six years before making a convert. He spent eighteen months in prison, but Ann smuggled papers to him so that he could continue translating the Bible. Soon after his release he saw Ann and their child die of spotted fever but he kept on working. Inspired in part by his mission, soon every American denomination was beginning to send missionaries overseas. By the end of the century Burma had sixty-three churches, with some seven thousand baptized converts. Thousands of others were being converted on every inhabited continent.

At the beginning of the period, Protestant Christianity was confined to Europe and its colonies. By its end Protestantism had become a worldwide religion. It is true that missionaries were sometimes too much the agents of the colonialism that exploited peoples. But it is also true that missionaries were leaders in protesting that exploitation, and all over the world they founded churches, hospitals, and schools.

The Sunday School

The Second Great Awakening and worldwide mission activity went hand in hand with the Sunday school. Sunday school missionaries made their contribution to the spread of the gospel throughout the American frontier.

Sometime in 1780 or 1781 a godly woman is said to have stormed into the office of the editor of the *Journal,* the daily newspaper in Gloucester, England, and said in effect, "Your efforts at prison reform come too late. What we need is to reach these kids before they have to go to jail." Anglican layman Robert Raikes, the editor, had used the *Journal* to crusade for many worthy causes. Now he employed four teachers, paid them a shilling per Sunday, and sent them to "Sooty Alley." There they began to teach "the four Rs" (reading, writing, arithmetic, and religion) to children who worked in the mills and factories the other six days of the week. The Sunday school was born.

It spread with amazing rapidity. Five years later a Baptist dealer in cloth led in forming the first organization of Sunday schools, "to prevent vice, to encourage industry and virtue, to dispel the ignorance of darkness, to diffuse the light of knowledge, to bring men cheerfully to submit to their stations." By 1787 it was estimated that a quarter of a million children were enrolled. Frightened by the French Revolution, the archbishop of Canterbury denounced Sunday schools as "nurseries of fanaticism," and only with difficulty was Prime Minister William Pitt persuaded not to introduce in Parliament a bill prohibiting this dangerous innovation.

By about 1800 Sunday schools spread to America. In 1830 the American Sunday School Union launched a campaign to "establish a Sunday School in every destitute place where it is practicable throughout the valley of the Mississippi." They defined that valley as everything from Harrisburg, Pennsylvania, to the Rocky Mountains. Gifts poured in to support the work. In many communities the union Sunday school was established first, with the denominational churches coming later.

If, some time after 1824, you had attended Sunday school you might have been given a card containing fifteen rules:

1. I must always mind the Superintendent and all the Teachers of this School.
2. I must come every Sunday, and be here when School goes in.
3. I must go to my seat as soon as I come in.

4. I MUST ALWAYS BE STILL.
. . . .
15. I, [name], *must always mind the Superintendents and all the Teachers of this school.*[1]

You would have sung songs, among them, perhaps, "Death of a Pious Child," "Death of a Scholar," and "For a Dying Child." In the first part of the nineteenth century children were often in the home where someone was dying, and many died in childhood.

The Sunday school established libraries. By 1859 it was estimated that out of fifty thousand libraries in this country thirty thousand were established under Sunday school auspices. Scripture was the curriculum, and memorization was required. If you were a boy you might through hard work win a prize, a book entitled *An Authentic Account of the Conversion, Experience, and Happy Deaths of Twelve Boys.* If you were a girl you might win a book about the deaths of thirteen girls.

Of the early Sunday school books the one that was to have the most lasting and widespread effect was called *Say and Seal.* It was written by two Presbyterian Sunday school teachers, Anna and Susan Warner. It described the death of little Johnny Fax. Faith, his Sunday school teacher, and John Linden, her suitor, would rock the dying child and sing to him. Near the end of the story he stretches out his bony arms and pleads, "Sing." Now for the first time John sings:

Jesus loves me, this I know, / For the Bible tells me so;
Little ones to him belong, / They are weak but he is strong.

Jesus loves me—he who died, / Heaven's gate to open wide;
He will wash away my sin, / Let his little child come in.

Jesus loves me, loves me still, / Though I'm very weak and ill;
From his shining throne on high, / Comes to watch me where I lie.

Jesus loves me—he will stay / Close beside me all the way.
Then his little child will take / Up to heaven for his dear sake.

As Johnny dies, listening to his favorite verses from Revelation, John Linden says, "We were permitted to show him the way at first, Faith, but he is showing it to us now."[2]

Not long afterward, someone added a bouncy chorus to that lugubrious song:

Yes, Jesus loves me! / Yes, Jesus loves me!
Yes, Jesus loves me! / The Bible tells me so!

The mood of the country, following the Civil War, was changing. Children were no longer so often dying in infancy. Congregational pastor Horace Bushnell was teaching many that the task of the church was more to nurture children for this life than to help them prepare for heaven.

In 1872 a Baptist layman and a Methodist minster helped produce the first Uniform Lesson selection of Scripture passages. The American Sunday School Union adopted them. Thus most Sunday schools of most denominations studied the same Scripture passage in all classes each Sunday, a kind of Protestant lectionary. In the 1890s many Sunday schools began organizing classes for adults.

It is important to note that the Sunday school from the beginning until the present has been a lay movement. The pastor might dominate the worship service, but, as one historian puts it, the Sunday school has been "the people's church." Equally important, though women might be excluded from the ministry of Word and sacrament, women found a place of leadership in the Sunday school.

The Civil War

One teacher of children had not fared well. In 1787, in Charleston, South Carolina, George Daugheday, a Methodist minister, was drenched in public cistern water. His crime: he had been teaching children of slaves.

The American church had never been quite sure what to do about slavery. The view of many thoughtful southerners, such as Washington and Jefferson, was that slavery was wrong and should be eliminated. (Washington's will freed his slaves, though Jefferson's did not.) They felt that emancipation should be gradual, and that it would inevitably take place voluntarily over the years. Beginning in 1817 the American Colonization Society raised funds for resettling freed slaves in Africa; that resettling led to the founding of the Republic of Liberia. In the meantime men like Washington and Jefferson, otherwise facing bankruptcy, kept their slaves throughout their lifetimes. Most church bodies accepted this approach, calling slavery evil but warning that sudden emancipation might produce disastrous results for both races and that the church should not become involved in pronouncements on political matters that might split the nation and produce bloodshed.

Nevertheless, some Christians were determined to stir the conscience of the nation to overcome this evil. Charles Finney called for the church to take a stand against slavery, confident that preaching the gospel would cause Christians to free their slaves. Theodore Dwight Weld's books helped raise abolitionist sentiments. *Uncle Tom's Cabin*, by Congregationalist Harriet Beecher Stowe, aroused emotions on both sides. In 1844 both the Methodist and the Baptist denominations split, primarily over slavery. In the war of 1861–65 the issue of slavery itself was settled, but the victims of slavery received little justice, and the still dominant whites had no less prejudice against their African American neighbors.

African American Denominations

If you had been a slave prior to the war you might have been a baptized and fully enrolled member of a Methodist, Baptist, Episcopal, or Presbyterian church. You would have been required to sit, however, in a slave gallery, segregated from your master. The preacher would from time to time exhort you, emphasizing the words of Paul, "Servants, be obedient to your masters according to the flesh, with fear and trembling" (Eph. 6:5, King James Version). More likely, your worship would have been in a group of fellow slaves exhorted by a slave preacher. If you were like other African Americans you would have responded enthusiastically to the gospel. The spirituals you sang would become America's greatest contribution to the world's literature of worship.

After the war most denominations attempted to minister to African Americans, sometimes seeking to keep them in their prewar congregations or themselves setting up black congregations. A few congregations for free blacks had been formed earlier, but it was following the war that most of the separate African American denominations were developed. Methodists and Baptist groups were most successful. Founded in the north even before the war, the African Methodist Episcopal Church and the African Methodist Episcopal Zion Church began to minister to southern blacks. Black Methodists founded the Colored Methodist Episcopal Church, later named the Christian Methodist Episcopal Church. Black Baptists formed congregations, and many of these joined to establish the National Baptist Convention. The Church of God in Christ was founded in Memphis in 1897, under the leadership of C. H. Mason and Charles Price Jones. It later divided, as Mason became an enthusiast of a new and growing movement, Pentecostalism.

The Pentecostal Movement

It was a black minister, William J. Seymour, who led in what was to become one of the most far-reaching movements in the history of Protestantism, extending into the twenty-first century. In 1906 blacks and whites together began to flock to an abandoned Methodist church on Azusa Street in Los Angeles. A special aspect of the Azusa Street revival was that many began to "speak in tongues." Seymour and others believed that this phenomenon was a return of Pentecost as described in the second chapter of Acts and that it probably portended the beginning of the end of the world. In Pentecostal worship many might speak at once, often in words that no one else understood but that were believed to be given by the Spirit. Women were often leaders. The sick reported that they had been healed. New songs expressed heartfelt gratitude to God.

One Pentecostal denomination, the Assemblies of God, made up largely of people whose ancestors had come from England and other northern European countries, was founded in 1914. By the beginning of the twenty-first century it had enrolled more than 2,500,000 members and was still growing. The Pentecostal Holiness Church spread among all races, but especially among blacks and Hispanics. The movement found fertile soil in South America and Africa, winning millions of adherents on those two continents. By the middle part of the twentieth century, President John A. Mackay of Princeton Theological Seminary suggested that one should speak not of a twofold division of the church around the world, Protestant and Catholic, but of three: Protestant, Catholic, and Pentecostal.

From time to time Pentecostalism has arisen in the older, traditional denominations. Roman Catholic Pentecostals have usually become more loyal to their church. Among Protestants Pentecostalism has sometimes caused division, as groups of members, feeling that they had received the Holy Spirit while their pastors and others had not, withdrew to form independent congregations.

Some Other New Movements and Denominations

The nineteenth century saw the birth of a number of denominations. John Wesley had greatly emphasized holiness in life and had taught that perfection was possible, though he made no claim to have achieved it himself. Some Methodists felt that Wesley's concern had been forgotten and that the Methodist Church had become worldly. They split off to form a basis for several "Holiness" denominations. Some groups became heirs of both the Pentecostal and Holiness movements. Others, like the Church of the Nazarene, rejected Pentecostalism but emphasized the strict and holy life.

On March 21, 1843, thousands of Christians gazed into heaven looking for the second advent, the return of Christ. Some even climbed a mountain to be the first to greet the Savior. When that expectation failed, their leader, William

Miller, revised his understanding of biblical prophecy and set a new date, October 22, 1844. Though that too failed, several "Adventist" denominations came into being, the largest being the Seventh-day Adventists, led by Ellen White. Obeying literally the fourth commandment (Deut. 5:12–15), they observe Saturday as their day of rest.

In the chaotic days prior to the First World War, Charles T. Russell denounced three things as instruments of Satan: government, business, and the church. He predicted that the world would end in 1914. The world did not end in 1914, but World War I did begin, a sign, some proposed, that Satan had been cast out of heaven onto the earth. They did not forget the promise that many then living would never die but welcome Christ's second advent. Under the leadership of Joseph F. Rutherford, a lawer, the new denomination carried on, named by him "Jehovah's Witnesses." They continued to be so sure that the end was near that only near the end of the twentieth century did their highly successful publication *The Watchtower* announce that it was not a sign of lack of faith in the imminence of Christ's second coming for Jehovah's Witnesses to buy life insurance.

These groups were premillennialist. That is, they believed that Christ was coming again, probably quite soon, and then would set up a kingdom here on earth for a millennium, a thousand years. This view, based on a literal reading of Revelation 20, was by no means confined to organized premillennial sects. Thousands saw Mussolini as the beast of Revelation 13:18, and when his power faded ingenious methods were used to show that Hitler was Revelation's beast whose number is 666. In the 1970s Hal Lindsey's *Late Great Planet Earth* became a best seller, warning, in the title of his next book, that people then might be living in *The Terminal Generation.* Outselling all in the 1990s was a series of novels by Tim LaHaye and Jerry B. Jenkins, begun with *Left Behind.* Based on their understanding of 1 Thessalonians 4:16–17, these books professed to describe the seven years of miseries on earth they thought would come upon those who were not "raptured" up to heaven at Christ's second coming. Rather than the experience of the troubles that Revelation warns Christians must go through, these novels offered a way of escape to heaven through faith in the coming Christ. These books continued to sell in the tens of millions into the twenty-first century. All predictions of the time of the end have had one thing in common: they have all proved false.

The most clearly unique American denomination is the Church of Jesus Christ of Latter-day Saints, often called "Mormons." Joseph Smith announced that an angel had enabled him to read a collection of golden tables, written in Egyptian hieroglyphics, which he dictated to a group of followers. To the Mormons this *Book of Mormon,* published in 1830, became a second Bible, as important as the first. The Mormons denied the traditional doctrine of the Trinity, describing instead three separate beings. They so emphasized marriage that men were encouraged to take more than one wife; they performed baptisms for the dead. Christ, they taught, had come to America, and the Native Americans were related to the "ten lost tribes" of Israel. Mormons began calling Smith "King of the kingdom of God." Angered by his advocating polygamy, an Indiana mob lynched him. One of the most remarkable stories of heroic steadfastness to faith is that of the trek of the Mormons to Utah. There they set up a Mormon community and began to send out missionaries. By the beginning of the twenty-first century they had abandoned polygamy, had founded Brigham Young University, and, with pairs of door-to-door evangelists spreading their faith, had been able to claim some nine million adherents, all over the world.

Appealing more to the upper middle class, in 1879 Mary Baker Eddy founded the Church of Christ, Scientist. Suffering from repeated illness, she came to believe that she was cured by believing that illness is error, not materially real. The Christian Scientist was not to go to doctors or to take medicines but to read Eddy's writings and understand the unreality of evil. By the end of the twentieth century her book *Science and Health, with a Key to the Scriptures* had been printed some four hundred times. It promised happiness and prosperity to all who followed its teachings. As she grew older, she herself, however, became more and more dependent on morphine and on her friends, whose attentions protected her from the waves of "animal magnetism" of her enemies.

New Social Concern

While Adventists were pointing toward the end of this world and Christian Scientists were focusing on the inner spiritual life, many, especially of the mainline denominations, were taking a new interest in making this present material world a better place.

In 1907 a Baptist professor named Walter Rauschenbusch published *Christianity and the Social Crisis,* and he followed it with other works, including *A Theology of the Social Gospel.* As a young pastor he had served a church not far from New York's Hell's Kitchen. His experience with the poor and with laboring people had led him to new concerns. He considered himself an orthodox Christian, not denying traditional tenets of the faith, but he proposed that the church had failed to emphasize certain other ideas that were equally implied by the gospel. The cry for social justice voiced by Amos and other Old Testament prophets was needed in twentieth-century America. The church, he argued, must recognize sin in terms not simply of such things as dancing and playing cards but of sweatshops, slums, and the mass slaughter of war. Salvation must be understood not only as the conversion of individuals but as progress of society toward the justice and fellowship that he saw as the nature of the kingdom of God. He saw Jesus' death not so much in terms of vicarious atonement bringing individuals salvation as in Jesus' war against the sins that caused that death, sins such as religious bigotry, political corruption, and mob action. His "social gospel," championed by other writers and thousands of preachers, influenced seminaries and denominational agencies. Mission boards began to place more emphasis on building educational institutions and hospitals and helping people of poor nations with economic development, less on rescuing individual sinners from hell.

The works of Rauschenbusch "left an indelible print"on the thinking of a young black Baptist pastor named Martin Luther King Jr. On December 1, 1955, on a city bus in Montgomery, Alabama, Rosa Parks refused to relinquish her seat to a white passenger. King found himself heading a boycott that eventually ended segregation on Montgomery's buses. In Selma, Birmingham, Atlanta, and other cities, King's Southern Christian Leadership Conference helped mobilize African Americans in nonviolent demonstrations. African American churches became the home base for many protest marches and restaurant sit-ins that helped overturn segregation laws in many places and persuaded Congress to pass the Voting Rights Act of 1965, guaranteeing all races the right to vote. Some white Christians joined in; some southern white congregations posted Sunday morning "temple guards" to stop blacks from entering. Many southern pastors, confessing their sympathy with the cause of racial justice, were forced from their pulpits. In New York thousands of whites joined in as King led a massive march protesting the Vietnam War. King also began to argue that blacks were the victims of an economic system that kept them in poverty.

Many denominational agencies endorsed such movements for racial justice. Many took stands calling for cutting back on armaments and protesting American support of corrupt dictatorships in Latin America and Africa. Such stands helped produce a conflict between the ordinary laypeople and their denominational leadership. To many conservative church members it seemed that their church courts, far from representing their views, were moving toward endorsing racial unrest, labor policies that threatened their businesses, and the communism that seemed to be sweeping Asia and that Senator Joseph McCarthy had warned was growing in the American church and state. Something of this distrust continued into the twenty-first century, fueled anew by debates over such issues as the place of women, abortion, Bible in the schools, and homosexuality.

Fundamentalism and Evangelicalism

Equally alarming to many was the biblical and theological liberalism of the denominational seminaries and agencies. To some it seemed that sin and salvation were being defined only in terms of social reform. New interpretations of Scripture also seemed to threaten tradition. Luther and Calvin had insisted that the Bible should be interpreted in the light of the historical circumstances in which a given book was written. Now such study led many to conclude that the Pentateuch was written long after Moses and that many stories in Scripture, however inspired, could not be regarded as historical fact. The theory of evolution was being accepted rather than the seven-day creation described in Genesis. When in 1951 the Revised Standard Version of Scripture first appeared in 1951, extreme conservatives, reared on the King James Version and fearing, for example, that the use of the words "young woman" in the this new translation of Isaiah 7:14 was a denial of Jesus' virgin birth, made public bonfires of this new "liberal" Bible.

Reacting to twentieth-century changes in the world, and to what some regarded as progress but which seemed to them to be decay of the faith, some Christians urged emphasis on what they defined as the "fundamentals" of Christian doctrine. These included the inerrancy of Scripture, the virgin birth of Christ, the substitutionary theory of the atonement, Jesus' bodily resurrection, and his coming visible return. To fundamentalists, only those who could pass these doctrinal tests were orthodox Christians. Conservative—as they saw it—in their theology, many fundamentalists allied themselves politically with the right wing of the Republican Party. In 1988 fundamentalist television evangelist Pat Robertson ran for the Republican nomination for the presidency, and, though he did not win, many Republican candidates have been careful to champion some causes fundamentalists espouse, such as limiting abortion, support for Israel, limits on gay rights, and prayer in the public schools. By the end of the twentieth century fundamentalists were in control of the mission board and the denominational seminaries of the Southern Baptists, the largest Protestant denomination.

Many who agreed with the fundamentalists' doctrines perceived the term "fundamentalism" as having connotations of narrowness and intolerance. They claimed for themselves instead the name "evangelicals." (From the Reformation until this development "evangelicals" had been used of all Protestants who taught salvation through faith in Christ.) They emphasized religious experience such as personal conversion and awareness of God's continuing care. Their scholars produced new translations of the Bible, including the New International Version. Through television and preaching campaigns evangelical Billy Graham preached to millions.

Many evangelical congregations began to emphasize heartfelt worship, and, often inspired by simple, rhythmical choruses, their worship focused on joy in salvation. The words were frequently projected on screens rather than found in hymnals, and strings and drums replaced organs in their "praise services." Many congregations not fundamentalist in theology adopted some of these practices for one worship service each Sunday. Some fundamentalists felt constrained to leave their denominations to form new ones or to join independent congregations.

Cooperative and Ecumenical Movements

It would be a mistake, however, to think of the nineteenth and twentieth centuries as a time simply of the formation of new sects and the division of old denominations. Christians repeatedly found ways of cooperating across sectarian lines. We have noted the cooperative work of the American Sunday School Union. Abolitionist societies included men and women of many groups. The Young Men's Christian Association and the Young Women's Christian Association built up youth both spiritually and physically. Originated in England, the Salvation Army became Protestantism's most effective ministry among the poor. The Women's Christian Temperance Union led the fight against alcohol. Their success in pushing for the Eighteenth Amendment, forbidding the sale of alcoholic beverages, showed that women were capable of political action. Thus the movement for women's suffrage gained strength. Women, having won the vote, began more and more to demand ordination as ministers, and by the end of the twentieth century they had won that battle in most of the mainline denominations.

Denominations that had split in the nineteenth century began to reunite. Methodists north and south reunited in 1939, and in 1968 they united with the Evangelical United Brethren to form the United Methodist Church, second in size among Protestant bodies only to the Southern Baptists. Earlier the Evangelical and Reformed Church had brought together churches growing out of the Swiss and German Reformed movements. In 1957 the spiritual descendants of the New England Puritans, called the Congregational Christian Church, united with them to form the United Church of Christ. By 1983 the largest Presbyterian bodies had reunited too, bringing together what thirty years before had been three branches of that family. Lutherans had come to this country in large numbers especially in the latter half of the nineteenth century. They were divided by the languages and customs of many northern European nations. Gradually these diverse groups drew together, and in 1987 several Lutheran denominations merged to form the Evangelical Lutheran Church, the largest Lutheran body in America.

The ecumenical movement encouraged biblical scholars and theologians of different denominations to learn from one another. Two world wars had dealt a severe blow to the optimistic view of some liberals that the goodness of human nature was enabling us to progress toward the kingdom of God. Neo-orthodoxy, derived in part from the German and Swiss thinkers Karl Barth and Emil Brunner, reemphasized in new ways a Calvinistic awareness of the sinfulness of human nature. Though still accepting modern historical criticism, many in once more liberal seminaries now emphasized that the Bible is not just the record of the religious experience of one group of people; it is the Holy Spirit's unique witness to the one true Word of God, Jesus Christ, God's gracious revelation of the divine self to sinful humanity.

The twentieth century's ecumenical movement brought denominational families together. In 1908 thirty-nine denominations, black and white, formed the Federal Council of Churches, especially concerned to work for justice in society. It in turn merged with other ecumenical bodies to create the National Council of Churches. Through it, many mainline Protestant denominations continue to share insights concerning Christian education, carry on Church World Service, cooperate with Habitat for Humanity, take united stands concerning issues of racial and economic justice, and work for peace. Following the tragic bombing of the World Trade Center, Sept. 11, 2001, it developed new programs to promote good relations with Muslims, often victims of new prejudice.

In the nineteenth century Roman Catholicism had moved further from Protestantism, proclaiming the immaculate conception of Mary herself and, when he defines doctrine ex cathedra, the infallibility of the pope. In 1962, however, the Second Vatican Council, called by Pope John XXIII, opened up a new day of conversation and cooperation between Catholics and Protestants.

As a symbol of twenty-first-century ecumenism, growing out of the earlier Consultation on Church Union, in 2002 thirty-six mainline denominations joined in a fellowship called Churches Uniting in Christ. At this writing this group attempts only to promote intercommunion among its member denominations, not their organic union. It shows, however, that many churches in the twenty-first century dream that someday the visible body of Christ will be more nearly one again in organization, even as it has always been in the Spirit.

Some American Christians' Thoughts

Perhaps the true story of Christianity is shown more clearly in quotations from leading Christians than in accounts of church divisions and unions. One of the most colorful of the nineteenth-century crusaders was Sojourner Truth. She escaped from slavery and began to preach to crowds her twin concerns of freedom for African Americans and for women. Among her most famous addresses is "Ain't I a Woman?" Here are some excerpts:

> That man over there says that women need to be helped into carriages, and lifted over ditches, and to have the best place everywhere. Nobody ever helps me into carriages, or over mud-puddles, or gives me any best place! And ain't I a woman? Look at me! Look at my arm! I have ploughed and planted, and gathered into barns, and no man could head me! And ain't I a woman? I could work as much and eat as much as a man—when I could get it—and ain't I a woman? I have borne thirteen children, and seen most all sold off to slavery, and when I cried out with my mother's grief, none but Jesus heard me! And ain't I a woman? . . . Then that little man in black there, he said women can't have as much rights as men, 'cause Christ wasn't a woman! Where did your Christ come from? . . . From God and a woman! Man had nothing to do with Him. If the first woman God ever made was strong enough to turn the world upside down all alone, these women together ought to be able to turn it back, and get it right side up again! And now they is asking to do it, the men better let them.[3]

The ecumenical movement developed out of world missions. Methodist John R. Mott became a leader in the YMCA and headed the Student Volunteer Movement for Foreign Missions. At the influential Edinburgh Missionary Conference of 1910 Mott preached:

> It is a startling and solemnizing fact that even as late as the twentieth century, the Great Command of Jesus Christ to carry the Gospel to all mankind is still so largely unfulfilled. . . . The church is confronted today, as in no preceding generation, with a literally world wide opportunity to make Christ known.

Mott's great theme was "The Evangelization of the World in This Generation." His goal was not achieved, but the Student Volunteer Movement inspired thousands of young women and men to give their lives in missionary service.

The most influential American-born theologian of the twentieth century was Reinhold Niebuhr of Union Theological Seminary in New York. His Calvinistic heritage helped move him from the liberals' optimism to realistic warning against the injustice seemingly inherent in society. One statesman influenced by Niebuhr was President Jimmy Carter. Not all agreed with President Carter's particular programs aimed at peace and social justice, but his subsequent work with Habitat for Humanity and the Carter Foundation's efforts for peace and justice around the world have won near universal admiration. This Baptist layman, a Sunday school teacher, writes:

At its highest, government aspires to embody and defend values that are shared with religion. . . . Reinhold Niebuhr said, "To establish justice in a sinful world is the whole sad duty of the political order. There has never been justice without law; and all laws are the stabilization of certain social equilibria, brought about by pressures and counter-pressures in society, and expressed in the structures of government. . . ." Niebuhr's point is that the highest possible goal of a government or a society is justice: to treat people fairly, to guarantee their individual rights, to guard against discrimination, to try to resolve arguments peacefully. . . . That's what a government should do.[4]

Feminist theologian Rosemary Radford Ruether, critical of many pronouncements of the Roman Catholic Church such as the infallibility of the pope and the prohibition of women from the clergy, remains a loyal Catholic. She writes:

Jesus' vision of the Kingdom is neither nationalistic nor other-worldly. The coming Reign of God is expected to happen on earth, as the Lord's Prayer makes evident (God's kingdom come, God's will be done on earth). . . . The root idea of Christ is not that of personal and other-worldly salvation, but of social and historical salvation from the massive contradiction of collective human apostasy. This is the meaning of Jesus's [sic] crucifixion; not a deterministic "self-sacrifice" for individual "sins," but a political assassination on the cross of collective apostasy by the political and religious institutions that claim authority over our lives.[5]

No one else has ever preached to as many people as Billy Graham. He preached Jesus' self-sacrifice for individuals' sins, and hundreds of thousands responded to his evangelistic call. On the last night of his June 2001 campaign in Louisville the crowd of 57,000 read these words on the event's program:

Let us leave as an army of compassionate people. Let us proclaim Christ and His love as the answer to the deepest human need. If millions of Christians around the world would dare to demonstrate the love of Christ in every area of their lives, some of the alarming trends we see could well be reversed.[6]

Perhaps the twenty-first century will see something of that dream fulfilled.

Questions Chapter 8

1. From the revivals of Jonathan Edwards, Charles Finney, and on down to Billy Graham, Presbyterians have never been quite sure how to respond to the idea of evangelistic meetings. How do you think your congregation should be spreading the gospel to people who are not Christians?

2. What interested you most in this chapter's account of the history of the Sunday school?

3. What lessons must the church learn for today from the horrors of slavery and the Civil War, and from the church's failures in relation to them?

4. This chapter notes the development of "the social gospel." When is it proper for church courts to take stands on great controversial social and political issues such as civil rights or abortion?

5. What experience have you had with people who speak with tongues? with devotees of the *Left Behind* series and others who try to see current events as showing that the end of the world is at hand? What can the rest of us learn from them?

6. What changes might the church make in the nation and the world today more efficiently if it were not so splintered by now irrelevant conflicts? What hope do you see for the church's union, for which Christ prayed (John 17:11)?

Chapter 9

Presbyterians in America
(c. 1650–Present)

*I*n 1672 in Jamaica, Long Island, New York, a group of immigrants from Scotland banded together to form a church. Presbyterianism had begun to take root in the New World.

The Jamaica congregation were not the first Presbyterians to arrive. Some Huguenots had settled in Florida by 1562. Others came to Charleston, South Carolina. In 1628 the Dutch Reformed Church, Calvinist in doctrine and Presbyterian in government, had been established in New Amsterdam, with James Michaelius as its first pastor. The Reformed Church in America continues to be a vigorous denomination, together with its sister church of Dutch Calvinist origins, the Christian Reformed Church. The Jamaica church, however, is probably correct in claiming to be the oldest permanent congregation in the United States bearing the name "Presbyterian."

Chapter 7 included a brief account of the stand for religious freedom by Francis Makemie. Commissioned as a missionary by his presbytery in Ireland, he preached and helped organize churches up and down the coast, and in 1706 he and six other ministers formed the first presbytery. Soon Samuel Davies began organizing churches in Hanover County in Virginia, and with Hanover Presbytery Presbyterianism grew in the south.

The great growth of Presbyterianism in the colonies came from the immigration of the Scotch-Irish in the 1700s. Actually the Scotch-Irish were not Irish at all. James I had set out to solve "the Irish problem" by slaughtering rebellious Irish subjects or driving them out from Ulster (northern Ireland), and resettling Ulster with people from England, Wales, and Scotland. Thousands of Scots took advantage of the offer of cheaply rented land, and they brought the Presbyterian Church with them. Queen Anne, however, reversed that policy, raising the rent and placing severe restrictions and heavy taxes on these settlers. Forced by these economic pressures, beginning about 1715 Scots from Ulster began immigrating to America by the thousands. By the time of the American Revolution, Presbyterians were in size second only to the Congregationalists, the spiritual descendants of the Puritans who had come to New England. The first General Assembly of the Presbyterian Church, U.S.A., met in Philadelphia in 1789.

Worship in an Eighteenth-Century Congregation

If you had worshiped in a Presbyterian church about 1750 you would have sat in the pew you had rented in a simple, unadorned building.[1] The service would begin at 9:00 or 10:00 a.m. High above you, gazing down at you from his pulpit, you would see the gowned, bewigged minister. Just below him would be a lower pulpit, occupied by the song leader. He would slowly line out the psalm; that is, he would slowly sing a line and then the congregation would slowly sing it back. Only psalms were sung, and organs were regarded as "the devil's band." The minister would lead the morning prayer, which often went longer than twenty minutes, with the congregation standing. If you peeked during the prayer, you might spy young people slyly communicating with each other rather than with the Lord. From time to time such conduct, including laughing or any other kind of levity in the house of the Lord, was denounced.

Next came a lecture, an exposition of the Scripture for the sermon, taking up to half an hour. After another psalm there would be the sermon. The typical Presbyterian homily was, itself, by modern standards somewhat more like a lecture than a sermon. The minister would take a text, deduce from it a doctrine, and then expound that doctrine point by point, with many subheads under each point. Reading the sermon was frowned upon; ministers were encouraged to memorize. There would also be an application of the doctrine to your life. The sermon would take an hour or more. The service would include a collection for the poor. The whole service would take about two hours, sometimes more. After a fifteen-minute intermission for lunch, there would be another two-hour service with prayers, lecture, and sermon.

Worship would be carried on, however, not only on the Sabbath but throughout the week in your home. As a good Presbyterian father you were expected to lead the family each day in family prayers. As a good Presbyterian mother you and your husband would require your children to memorize the Westminster Shorter Catechism, and you would teach them the Bible. The minister or an elder might visit from time to time to test them, making sure that you were doing your job as parents.

The high point of the year would be the celebration of the Lord's Supper. Presbyterians would never have an *altar* for offering Christ's broken body again as a sacrifice to God, as in the mass. Instead Presbyterians would have a *table,* around which the faithful would share the Lord's Supper. Calvin had advocated that the sacrament be observed every Sunday, but eighteenth-century American Presbyterians preferred to make it a more special event. It was eagerly anticipated. There would be preparation for weeks. Often several congregations in the area would gather together. The celebration might go on for three days, even five, a great time of social as well as religious fellowship. If the crowds were too big for the church building, services might be outdoors, and the crowds might eat together. Several preachers would preach, perhaps at the same time in different nearby locations. The session would distribute tokens only to those deemed worthy to receive the body and blood of Christ; only those with tokens could receive Communion. At the climax all would drink from one common cup "until sensibly refreshed." The camp meetings of later days, such as the one at Cane Ridge that helped stimulate the Second Great Awakening, grew out of such services.

You could be sure that your minister was sound in the faith. Just how strictly ministers would be required to hold to every phrase of the Westminster Confession had been a matter for debate. The Adopting Act of 1729, however, had achieved a compromise. A minister was expected at ordination to affirm his acceptance of that confession. If he had any reservations, he must tell them to the presbytery. The presbytery must then determine if those reservations dealt with the essentials of the confession; and if, but only if, they were not matters they deemed essential, the presbytery might ordain him.

You could be sure that your pastor was a well-educated man. Though the College of New Jersey (later Princeton University) was never strictly under the government of the Presbyterian Church, the Presbyterians had been leaders in its establishment in 1746, and there many Presbyterian ministers were trained. From the beginning Presbyterians stressed education, and they soon founded more colleges.

Presbyterians and the Founding of the United States

"Cousin America has run off with a Presbyterian parson." So a member of the British Parliament is said to have lamented during the Revolutionary War.

Not all Presbyterians sided with the Revolution. Flora MacDonald was exiled with her family when she remained loyal to King George. But most Presbyterians were for independence. The Scots had warred with the English for centuries. Presbyterians had been the first in this country to establish themselves as a denomination independent of a mother church in Europe. Frontier folk liked to govern themselves. It is not surprising that Hanover Presbytery in Virginia became the first ecclesiastical body to declare for the Revolution. Presbyterians were to volunteer in large numbers for the army, and a number of the highest ranking officers were Presbyterians.

To say that the government of the United States was deliberately modeled on that of the Presbyterian Church would be a gross exaggeration. It is true, however, that the Calvinist concept of covenant, the experience of some American leaders in a church that was a kind of representative democracy, and the Presbyterian model of lower and higher courts did have influence.

If "Cousin America" had run off with one Presbyterian parson, that parson was the highly influential John Witherspoon. Famed on both sides of the Atlantic, he had reluctantly agreed to leave Scotland and become, in 1768, president of the College of New Jersey (later Princeton). He soon became a strong advocate of independence. Witherspoon was the only clergyman among the signers of the Declaration of Independence, and he was much involved in the proceedings of the Congress that produced it. When one delegate expressed fear that America was "not yet ripe" for independence, Witherspoon replied, "Sir, in my judgment the country is not only ripe for independence but in danger of rotting for want of it." He continued in the Congress for much of the Revolution. Equally important, at the college he taught not only religion but also such courses as ethics and philosophy, including political philosophy. Among Witherspoon's political views historian James A. Smylie notes these, which would seem to grow out of his Presbyterian Calvinism: (1) As sovereign, God alone, no king, can claim absolute authority. (2) Humans are so sinful they must have checks and balances. (3) God graciously provides government to curb our evil and promote good. (4) Human life in this world changes, and therefore a constitution should be flexible enough to meet changing conditions.[2]

Witherspoon's teaching had profound influence on many of his students. Young James Madison completed graduation requirements, but stayed on for another year because of his desire to study further under Witherspoon. Madison, of course, was to become known as "the Father of the Constitution." At one time or another Witherspoon taught his Presbyterian philosophy of government to many men who would become officeholders in the new republic, including a future president (Madison), a vice-president, nine cabinet officers, twenty-one senators, thirty-nine congressmen, three justices of the Supreme Court, and twelve state governors. Five of the signers of the Declaration had been this Presbyterian thinker's students.

Soon after the Revolution the question arose in Virginia concerning state support for its churches. It was proposed that each denomination be awarded

funds in relation to its size. Since except for the Episcopal Church the Presbyterians were the largest Virginia denomination, this would have been to the
Presbyterians' financial advantage. The Presbytery of Hanover, however,
resolved that it sought no state support, in effect endorsing the separation of
church and state for which Jefferson and Madison campaigned.

"Old School," "New School," and Cumberland Presbyterians

Americans were achieving freedom *of* religion. The General Assembly of
1798 noted, in effect, that too many seemed to be free *from* any religion. There
were said to be only four professing Christians at the Virginia Presbyterian
college Hampden-Sydney.

It was that little group, however, that helped trigger the Second Great
Awakening. In 1800 four Hampden-Sydney students began having prayer
meetings in their rooms. They were so ridiculed that the president of the college decided to invite them to his home for their next meeting. To his surprise,
his living room was crowded, and soon many were professing faith. A
preacher named James McGready went to see this phenomenon and stayed
for several days. A year later he was preaching at the Cane Ridge Camp Meeting the sermons that helped spread the revival message to thousands.

Presbyterians have never been quite sure what attitude to take toward
revivals. The first preachers and the most widely successful of the revival
preachers, McGready, Finney, and Lyman Beecher, were all Presbyterians for
at least part of their ministries. Revivals added thousands to the church, and
many, many lives were changed. Yet by 1832 the Assembly was warning that
"an undue excitement should be carefully avoided"[3] (italics in the original). The
jerks and barks and faintings of those caught up in horror for their sins seemed
to accord ill with the dignity of Presbyterian worship. It bothered many that
women were praying aloud in revival meetings. And the revivalists' demands
for decision seemed to some out of keeping with Calvin's doctrine of election
by God alone. In 1837 the denomination split, with "New School" Presbyterians supporting the revival and "Old School" Presbyterians urging caution.

McGready himself remained a Presbyterian all his life, but new denominations such as the Christian Church (Disciples of Christ) and the Churches
of Christ arose from the Second Great Awakening, and the revival helped
sever the Cumberland Presbyterians from the larger Presbyterian denomination. Two issues were involved. Several members of Cumberland Presbytery
acknowledged that they did not believe in double election, Calvin's doctrine
that God had from all eternity selected some individuals for salvation and

some for damnation. But also Cumberland Presbyterians were inspired by the goal of carrying the gospel to the frontier without waiting to send candidates for the ministry back east for a long program of education. It was not that they were opposed to education. In due time Cumberland Presbyterians organized many schools and colleges. Among those now related to the Presbyterian Church (U.S.A.) are Trinity University, Millikin College, the University of the Ozarks, Missouri Valley College, and Waynesburg College. Cumberland University is independent, and Bethel College and Memphis Theological Seminary remain institutions of the continuing Cumberland Presbyterian Church. But in the early 1800s the field seemed too white unto the harvest to permit waiting. In 1810, in Dickson County, Tennessee, in the log cabin of Presbyterian minister Samuel McAdow, the Cumberland Presbyterian Church was born.

The remaining Presbyterians were not of one mind. In 1741 Presbyterians had split over differences related to the First Great Awakening, into Old Side and New Side Presbyterians, though they had eventually reunited. Now in part because of differences growing out of the awakening, in 1837 Presbyterians divided again, into Old School and New School. Presbyterians and Congregationalists (today part of the United Church of Christ) had had a "Plan of Union," an alliance that enabled them to cooperate in missionary and benevolent activities. Those forming the Old School feared that the Congregationalists were no longer strict enough in their Calvinism. But underlying the differences was the question that would soon divide the whole nation, slavery. Many Presbyterian churches in the south favored the Old School.

The Civil War and Schism

In 1787 the Synod of New York and Philadelphia stated that it did "highly approve of the general principles in favor of universal liberty . . . yet . . ." instead of condemning slavery, as it had been asked to do, it settled for instructing masters to treat their slaves kindly and see that they attended the preaching of the gospel. After all, many Presbyterians reasoned, the Bible, our authority, never condemns slavery but seems at times to endorse it. In 1817 the General Assembly had recommended colonization of freed slaves in Africa and asked that every Fourth of July each church take up an offering for that cause. The 1836 Assembly, however, resolved that it could not bind the conscience of its members and recommended that the whole subject of slavery be indefinitely postponed.

The difference could not be disposed of that easily. New School Presbyterians divided in 1857. When in 1861 the Confederate States of America declared their independence, the Old School General Assembly declared that loyalty to the federal government was the duty of all Christians. Most southern churches withdrew, and the Presbyterian Church in the Confederate States of America was formed. That body would not equivocate concerning slavery. Its General Assembly of 1864 affirmed that "domestic servitude is of Divine appointment" and that it was the peculiar mission of the "Southern Church to conserve the institution of slavery."

Following the war there was some repentance among southern Presbyterians. They did not repent, however, so much of having owned slaves. Instead they repented having as a church taken a stand on a secular, political matter. "The spirituality of the church," many felt, demanded that the church as a body concern itself strictly with matters of the soul, not of politics.

Cumberland Presbyterians never divided. Soon after the end of the war the Old School and New School Presbyterians reunited, but the north-south schism would continue until 1983.

Presbyterians: Missionaries to the World

Behold the heathen wants to know
The Joy the gospel will bestow,
The exiled captive to receive
The Freedom Jesus has to give.[4]

Presbyterian General Assemblies split, but probably many ordinary church members saw little difference in their Sunday worship. What did enter the lives of many Presbyterians singing hymns like the one just quoted was a concern for missions in their own country and around the world. Here are just a few examples of nineteenth-century Presbyterian missionaries.

One of the most storied of Presbyterian missionaries to the west was Narcissa Whitman. In 1836 with her physician husband and a pair of fellow missionaries, Henry and Eliza Spalding, she honeymooned in a covered wagon on her way to fulfill her life's ambition: she would be a missionary to the Native Americans. At a pass on the Oregon Trail a monument celebrates Narcissa and Eliza as the first white women to cross the Rockies. A beautiful girl, Narcissa was famed for her long, auburn hair. In 1847 the Whitmans were martyred, with the "Indians" scalping Narcissa.

Among the most effective Presbyterian missionaries to the west was Sheldon Jackson. He was rejected by the foreign mission board as not healthy enough to work overseas. Determined that Presbyterians should do their share in carrying the gospel along the line of the new transcontinental railroad, during the 1870s Jackson traveled some thirty thousand miles annually, on foot, by stagecoach, ox cart, and railroad, planting and promoting missions. He himself organized schools and established churches, and his monthly newspaper publicizing mission work, the *Rocky Mountain Presbyterian*, gained a circulation of twenty thousand. In 1877 he moved on to Alaska, there traveling often by bobsled and even canoe. He helped found churches and mission schools, and his repeated appeals brought federal aid to establish public schools in the territory. His introduction of the reindeer to Alaska is said to have been the economic salvation of the native population. In total Jackson organized some one hundred churches. Sheldon Jackson College, a Presbyterian school in Sitka, Alaska, stands as one monument to his ministry.

Presbyterians were early in sending missionaries all over the world. Among the most colorful of missionaries was "the black Livingstone," Henry Sheppard. In 1890 the southern Presbyterians sent Sheppard with a white man, Samuel Lapsley, as a missionary to the Belgian Congo. A year later Lapsley died, but Sheppard carried on, exploring into unknown territory and preaching the gospel. Sheppard became widely known in the United States as he gave lectures to raise money for the mission. Here he often had to travel in the boxcar with the animals, since black people were not supposed to sit with white people on trains. King Leopold of Belgium encouraged genocidal tribal warfare to help secure his hold on the rubber business. Sheppard's protests caused his arrest and trial, and that in turn drew international attention to the exploitation of Africans by colonial powers.

Only two years after the war the southern Presbyterians began a mission in China. When a mob of the Boxer Rebellion banged on the door of a Presbyterian mission they were surprised to be answered by a young woman. Spreading out her arms as if to protect those inside, little Mary Morrow pleaded with the attackers to kill her but let the others go. They were so startled that at first they backed away, but soon they turned, hacked Mary Morrow to pieces, and slaughtered the others. Twenty years later the respected General Feng, once part of that mob, returned to that mission compound and asked to be baptized. He had never been able to erase from his mind the image of that heroic young martyr.

"Let your motto be resistance!" So, in 1883 in a public meeting, Henry Highland Garnet urged black Americans. He himself had escaped from slavery and had become pastor of Presbyterian churches in New York. He pleaded with the nation to be true to its Declaration of Independence, and he preached sermons comparing the slavery of blacks to that of the Israelites in Egypt. James W. C. Pennington, pastor of the First Colored Presbyterian Church of New York City, lectured on both sides of the Atlantic, telling of his days as a slave blacksmith before his escape. After the Civil War, however, especially in the south, where the African American population was strongest, Presbyterians generally were not willing to see blacks as equals. Black ministers could not sit with whites in presbytery. Segregated synods were formed. Presbyterians did found some educational institutions for blacks, and there were notable black Presbyterians, but far more than the Presbyterians the Baptists, Methodists, and Pentecostals built African American churches.

Space allows only these few examples of the early days of Presbyterian mission work. But in such diverse places as Liberia and Hong Kong Cumberland Presbyterians minister, and in almost every part of the globe Presbyterian (U.S.A.) missionaries still preach the gospel, teach, establish schools and hospitals, and work for the economic development of nations. One thing to note is that while women were barred from ordination, they could be sent to face martyrdom as missionaries.

Presbyterian Women

The Southern Presbyterian General Assembly of 1880 left no doubt about its stand concerning women. Citing scriptural prohibitions, they affirmed, "The introduction of women into our pulpits for the purpose of publicly expounding God's Word [is] an irregularity not to be tolerated." But though barred from any chance to vote in sessions or higher church courts, women exercised considerable influence in church affairs. Already in 1870 the Presbyterian Church, U.S.A. (the northern branch), had established the Women's Foreign Mission Society. In 1875 the Southern Presbyterian Assembly began commending local women's missionary societies. In "home missions," it was women who were the major support of the work of Sheldon Jackson. Funds raised by women's associations in each branch of the church caused denominational agencies to court their support. While forbidding women from discussing any question publicly in any congregation, the southern church's assembly of 1891 reaffirmed the right of women to meet "for mutual edification and comfort by pious conversation and prayer," and for raising money for missions. It was something of a breakthrough when the 1926 Southern Presbyterian Assembly affirmed the right of the president of the Women's Auxiliary to read her own report to that body, though it carefully warned that she must not participate in any discussions on the floor of the assembly. Though excluded from any direct voice in guiding the church's program, the women's societies formed such an effective adult educational program that women became—and still are—better informed about the denomination's program than most Presbyterian men.

Shall Woman Preach? The Question Answered—with her book by that title Louisa Woolsey proposed a resounding yes to her own question. In 1889 Nolin Presbytery of the Cumberland Presbyterian Church ordained Mrs.

Woolsey, who had already begun preaching in churches in that area. The Kentucky Synod ruled her ordination out of order but did not revoke it. The assembly refused to seat her when she came as an alternate commissioner. Her presbytery stood by her, however, and she continued to serve, the first woman to be ordained as a Presbyterian minister.

Finally in 1956 the northern church approved the ordination of women as ministers of Word and Sacrament, and in 1964 the southern church followed.

Christian Education

Though excluded from the ministry, women were free to teach children and other women in Sunday school. The monthly *National Sunday School Teacher* of December 1870 discussed "Shall the Superintendent Talk?" Yes, it answered, he should not simply be an administrator but should spend ten minutes each Sunday expounding his understanding of the lesson to the whole school. That lesson would of course be the International Uniform Lesson for that Sunday, taught in all classes. In 1894 the southern church's assembly agreed to sanction the use of graded lessons for children, but only as a supplement to the revered, Bible-centered Uniform Lesson series. Graded lessons reflected the new child-centered educational psychology of John Dewey and other educators; they attempted to relate Scripture to each stage of growth in the mind and life of the child. In the days when many died in childhood, lessons had sought to convert the child before it was too late. The graded lessons, instead, had the goal of nourishing each child to grow toward adulthood as a bud grows into a flower. In many churches they replaced the Uniform Lesson series. Once Sunday school songs had warned sinful children of approaching death. Now children happily chorused, "Jesus Wants Me for a Sunbeam."

In the 1890s adult classes became a standard part of Sunday school. The opening and closing "exercises" formed lay-led worship services that, for some, became a kind of alterative to the preacher-dominated "church" that followed.

One great boon to Christian education was the establishment of summer conferences. In 1897 the first Montreat, North Carolina, "Christian Assembly" gathered on a wooden platform under a canvass cover. Montreat is the oldest and largest Presbyterian conference center, north or south. Thousands, young and old, began flocking to it every summer. Stony Point, near New York, began educating and inspiring others. By the middle of the twentieth century many presbyteries were establishing their own conference centers as well, with programs for youth and adults and training for Sunday school teachers, ministers, and church officers.

Christian education began to produce professionals. The Presbyterian School of Christian Education was the first school in the country designed specifically to train directors of Christian education and other lay professionals. Seminaries began offering master's degrees in that field. At first these educators were women, and thus, though their training was about as rigorous as that of ministers of the Word and Sacrament, they had no access to ordination.

The nondenominational Christian Endeavor movement had stimulated many congregations to form fellowships for youth. Now each branch of Presbyterianism developed its own vigorous youth program.

Soon after World War II, new developments in theology stimulated the production of new curricula. The Presbyterian Church, U.S.A. (the northern branch), introduced its "Faith and Life Curriculum"; and in the 1960s the southern Presbyterians, in cooperation with the Cumberland Presbyterians, the Reformed Church in America, and the Moravians, developed their "Covenant Life Curriculum." These sought to combine the biblical emphasis of the Uniform Lessons with the psychological insights of the Graded Lessons and to shape both in the light of Presbyterian, Reformed theology as it was developing in the days of neo-orthodoxy.

Educator-theologian Dr. Sara Little described the Uniform Lessons as reflecting the older biblicism and, later, neo-orthodoxy. The Graded Lessons showed the effects of liberalism's awareness of psychology. The Covenant Life Curriculum of the 1960s, she proposed, sought the best of all the currents in theology, using a kind of Presbyterian adaptation of theologian Paul Tillich's "principle of correlation." Tillich had sought to show how the deepest questions of the human psyche are related to the answers proclaimed in the gospel. Always on the leading edge, early in the 1980s Dr. Little was recommending Presbyterian seminary professor George W. Stroup's *The Promise of Narrative Theology*.[5] The concept of narrative or story would become basic to the new curricula produced in the late 1990s.

Thus Presbyterian Christian education deliberately based itself on Presbyterian theology, though as the world changed that theology had been required to deal with new questions in new ways.

New Challenges and Theological Developments

"Is man an ape or an angel?" So Prime Minister Benjamin Disraeli is said to have challenged the British Parliament. "I, my Lords, am on the side of the angels!"

The Second Great Awakening's emphasis on decision had brought challenges to the traditional Presbyterian doctrine of double election. New biblical scholarship, imported in part from Germany, brought about a new crisis in understanding the Bible. Darwin seemed to show that the Genesis narrative of creation in seven days was false. The study of the Bible in the light of history, an idea Calvin had championed, began to demonstrate that the first five books of the Bible were not the work of Moses. Indeed, they were the product of centuries of revision and editing, beginning no earlier than 1000 BC and completed no earlier than the fifth century. Their value as history was seriously questioned.

American Presbyterians reacted in a variety of ways. One approach brought a heresy trial for Charles A. Briggs. Theologians at Princeton proclaimed the inerrancy of Scripture, arguing that if we could not trust the Bible in history and science then we would be left in doubt about its message of salvation too. Influenced by new interpretations of the Bible, Professor Briggs of Union Seminary in New York argued that these Princeton theologians were going far beyond the Westminster Confession. Though actually quite conservative in theology, Briggs was convicted of heresy and barred from the ministry of the northern branch of Presbyterianism. Farther south, Columbia Seminary professor Thomas Woodrow, uncle of the future president Thomas Woodrow Wilson, began to propose that God might have created the human *body* through evolution, though the human *soul* was quite unique. Furious attacks led to the southern assembly's condemning such teaching as heresy. Woodrow was supported by his presbytery and synod and became president of the future University of South Carolina, but he was widely regarded as an enemy of the faith.

The most publicized debate concerning evolution was the famous "monkey trial" of 1923. John T. Scopes was accused of violating Tennessee law by teaching evolution in the public school of the little town of Dayton. Three times the Democratic Party candidate for president, and a sometime candidate for moderator of the General Assembly, Presbyterian layman William Jennings Bryan agreed to testify. Not only newspapers but the new medium of radio carried stories of the trial. Shrewd criminal lawyer Clarence Darrow maneuvered Bryan into admitting that in the case of the sun standing still (Joshua 10:12–14) God might have adapted the divine language to the ancients' human understanding of the cosmos. It is said that the crowd gasped as they realized that Bryan, now only a few days before his death, had been unable to defend biblical inerrancy convincingly. Gradually seminaries began to reject fundamentalism.

Opposed to fundamentalism, liberalism had another reaction to the challenges of the new science and the new biblical scholarship. Shortly after the trial in Dayton a group of liberal ministers in the north signed the Auburn Affirmation, asserting what they regarded as fundamentals of the faith but rejecting the precise statements of these demanded by fundamentalists. Some Presbyterian devotees of Walter Rauschenbusch's "social gospel" thought theological debates not nearly as important as working for justice in the world. Indeed, the world seemed to be if not *evolving* at least *progressing* toward the kingdom of God, a world of justice and mercy and peace. The Bible itself could be interpreted as presenting a progressive revelation, from the storm God Judge in the Old Testament to the loving Teacher of the Sermon on the Mount in the New Testament. Liberals challenged Presbyterians to join in "building the kingdom."

Two world wars dealt a heavy blow to the liberal belief in progress and the goodness of human nature. Sigmund Freud opened a window on the lust and perversion embedded deep in the human psyche. Presbyterian thinkers once again began to emphasize Calvin's view of the sinfulness of human nature and that mortals' only hope was to trust in God. Neo-orthodoxy enabled theologians to combine a critical, historical approach to Scripture with what seemed still the essentials of traditional Presbyterianism. In the divisive 1960s, the northern branch adopted the Confession of 1967 affirming Presbyterian doctrine in terms of reconciliation. In 1984 the Cumberland Presbyterian Church adopted a confession comparable to Westminster in scope but defining sin and salvation more in terms of relationships rather than Westminster's emphasis on law and justification. In 1991 the newly formed Presbyterian Church (U.S.A.) adopted a whole book of confessions, including the Nicene and Apostles' Creeds, and the Reformation's Second Helvetic Confession, the Westminster Confession and Catechisms, and the Heidelberg Catechism. To those confessions and the Confession of 1967 they added the Barmen Declaration, drawn up in 1934 by a group of German Protestants, led by Karl Barth in protest against nationalistic "German Christians" as Hitler rose to power. The new denomination itself produced A Brief Statement of Faith, outlined by the triune benediction of 2 Corinthians 13:13. It briefly recounted and affirmed the biblical story, and, among other things, endorsed the ordination of women, spoke of God as like a mother as well as a father, and summoned Presbyterians to "hear voices of peoples long silenced" and to work for peace and justice around the world. Having a whole book of confessions bore witness to the denomination's awareness of how its doctrine had developed through the long story of church history.

Not all agreed with new developments in doctrine, and schisms developed, but also new unions occurred.

Disunion and Union

Two groups that had come from Scotland united in 1782 to form the Associate Reformed Presbyterian Church. A splinter group, however, refused to go into the union, and continued as the Associate Presbyterians. In that fellowship young John Adams Ramsay was nurtured. When, in the 1860s, he enrolled at the University of Indiana, there being no Associate church in Bloomington, he worshiped with Bloomington's United Presbyterian Church of North America. Upon his return for the Christmas holidays he was summoned to appear before the session of his church. His crime was "the sin of occasional hearing"; that is, he had been listening to sermons by the wrong kind of Presbyterian. He agreed to consider the session's admonition seriously. It seems unlikely, however, that he obeyed, since he subsequently married the United Presbyterian pastor's daughter. He was to become a minister in the southern Presbyterian Church, which in 1983 merged with the northern Presbyterians, who had already joined with the United Presbyterians.

That story of my grandfather illustrates two tendencies of Presbyterians, schismatic narrowness and Christian reunion. While some other denominations have put more emphasis on inner experience or on outer activity, Presbyterians have always given a high place to purity in theology. This has sometimes led, as with the splinter group of Associate Presbyterians, to schismatic examination of other Presbyterians' beliefs to detect heresy. It is an exaggeration, however, to suggest that Presbyterians believe they should love their enemies but hate their brothers and sisters. Calvin is quoted as saying that he would cross every sea if by doing so he could reunite the church. In spite of repeated schism, Presbyterians have also repeatedly sought such reunion, and have led in cooperation with other denominations.

In 1906, after the northern Presbyterians had modified their version of the Westminster Confession of Faith to affirm more clearly the love of God for all, a large part of the Cumberland Presbyterian Church reunited with the Presbyterian Church, U.S.A. Some Cumberland Presbyterians refused to enter the merger, and continue as a small but vigorous denomination today, repeatedly working in cooperation with their sister denomination the Presbyterian Church (U.S.A.). In 1958 the northern Presbyterians merged with the United Presbyterian Church of North America, itself a union of two Presbyterian denominations, to form the United Presbyterian Church in the United States of America. In 1983, with the singing of the doxology, that group united with the southern Presbyterians to form the Presbyterian Church (U.S.A.).

Following the pattern of its predecessors, this denomination has been a leader in the ecumenical movement. It has been a major participant in the National Council of Churches and the World Council of Churches and is part of Churches Uniting in Christ, which seeks to achieve intercommunion across denominational lines.

There have continued, however, to be schisms. In 1936 fundamentalist biblical scholar J. Gresham Machen, who had left the Princeton faculty to form

Westminster Theological Seminary, helped to lead in the formation of the Orthodox Presbyterian Church. That body also split, with the Bible Presbyterian Church forming another new denomination. In 1983 many southern Presbyterian congregations refused to become part of the Presbyterian Church (U.S.A.), some finding a home in the Presbyterian Church in America, which had earlier withdrawn from the southern church.

The reasons were not just that the dissidents distrusted Presbyterian leadership as too liberal theologically. Seminaries and church agencies were also taking liberal stands on social issues that were quite different from those of many of the laity.

Moral and Social Issues

From the days of John Calvin on, Presbyterian leaders have denounced various kinds of sin. The General Assembly of 1818 resolved that "the theater we have always considered as a school of immorality" and that "dancing steals away our precious time, dissipates religious impressions, and hardens the heart." Participation in temperance societies was endorsed in 1829. Repeatedly assemblies called for renewed observance of the Sabbath.

To put teeth in its pronouncements, in the nineteenth century church courts still undertook to discipline members. A session might simply not send a Communion token to a delinquent member, but more serious offenses often called for more direct action, tempered with compassion. Historian R. Douglas Brackenridge tells how in the Cumberland Presbyterian Church of McGregor, Texas, the session reinstated one "brother" and one "sister" when they both confessed their sin of adultery and professed their repentance. In Goshen, Texas, a member confessed to the session that he had indeed been drunk, but he was forgiven when he pleaded that he had been suffering from colic and his druggist had recommended whiskey.[6]

The accused could appeal. Dr. Ernest Trice Thompson tells how the session of Central Presbyterian Church, Atlanta, suspended a deacon. He had allowed his home to be the site of a party in which young people had engaged not only in square dancing but in round dancing. He assured the session that he had not intended this to happen, but that it had not been "lascivious." The synod reversed the excommunication as too harsh. In another case a member was reinstated, but only after appealing to the General Assembly. She had been excommunicated because, driven by poverty, she had taken a job as a telephone operator and was working on the Sabbath.[7] Assemblies urged kindness to slaves, but there are few, if any, records of sessions disciplining masters for cruelty.

In the early 1900s Presbyterian assemblies supported the temperance movement that eventuated in Prohibition. That campaign may have helped move the church toward focusing more on social justice than on individual morality.

The National Council of Churches issued statements in behalf of organized labor and protesting working conditions in many mills. Particularly in the south, where many Presbyterians were in the mill-owner class, these elicited repeated demands from conservatives that the southern Presbyterian Church withdraw from that "communist-leaning" organization. Presbyterian assemblies protested the United States' support of oppressive dictators in Latin American countries, adding to the perception that the denomination's leaders were "soft on communism."

It was the civil rights movement, however, that brought the greatest conflict. Though the church had not officially called for change in the nation's "separate but equal" policy, it had more subtly undermined it. "In my Presbyterian Sunday school in Mississippi," one college student was saying in the 1940s, "we sang 'Jesus loves the little children . . . red and yellow, black and white,' and we had a picture of children of all races sitting at Jesus' feet. It made me wonder." A generation of Presbyterians were being prepared to accept change, though often grudgingly. Youth-led protests helped lead to the desegregation of Montreat.

In 1953 the southern Presbyterian General Assembly was the first national ecclesiastical body to issue a statement condemning segregation after the Supreme Court outlawed segregation in the public schools. Many congregations disapproved and some established "temple guards" to bar black "intruders" from their worship services. In Little Rock, Arkansas, Presbyterian Richard Hardie, with some other heroic white ministers and the session of his church, helped mobilize members to assist in defeating Governor Faubus's efforts to keep the schools segregated, and some persuaded their youth to welcome the black young people now attending Central High School. In Memphis some white Presbyterian ministers, "northern," "southern," and Cumberland, joined the protest march the day after Martin Luther King Jr. was assassinated there. It is difficult, decades later, to realize the courage that stand took in that place and time. As for black Presbyterians, they were likely to have crosses burned in their yards, and, when they demonstrated, to be beaten and jailed. A private Presbyterian fellowship was formed to aid the ministers throughout the South who were being forced to leave their churches because they spoke out in behalf of racial justice.

In 1968, after Martin Luther King's assassination, the southern Presbyterian Synod of Virginia announced that all who wished might be excused from attendance to travel on buses it had chartered to go to Washington, D.C., to participate in a march for the "Poor People's Campaign" that King had initiated. Highly financed attacks on such "political" stands and on denominational leadership helped spark schism. The Presbyterian Church in America separated from the southern Presbyterian Church in 1973, charging it with doctrinal stands that were too liberal and with improper involvement in political affairs.

When, in 1983, the southern and northern branches of the church reunited to form the Presbyterian Church (U.S.A.), some ten percent of the southern Presbyterians were allowed to withdraw, the biggest Presbyterian schism of the twentieth century. Many congregations joined the Presbyterian Church in America. The dissidents charged the Presbyterian Church (U.S.A.) with heresy, and protested the ordination of women. The Presbyterian Church (U.S.A.), however, has repeatedly demonstrated its loyalty to the theology of the Reformed tradition.

Presbyterian Worship in the Twenty-first Century

If somehow you had been transported from the eighteenth century worship service described at the beginning of this chapter to worship in a Presbyterian congregation today, in many churches the first difference you would notice is that the pastor might be a woman. You would see many other differences too.

In 1789 the presbytery of Transylvania inquired of the General Assembly whether it was true, as they felt, that the church had "fallen into a great and pernicious error" by singing not the Psalms but the hymns of Isaac Watts. True, these were loosely based on psalms; "Joy to the World" reflects Psalm 98. The assembly answered that Watts's hymns were appropriate. Singing from the hymnal of 1874 you could have joined in warning yourself and others:

> That awful day will surely come.
> The appointed hour makes haste,
> When I must stand before my Judge
> And pass a solemn test.[8]

In the 1920s you might have sung a hymn popularized in the Billy Sunday evangelistic campaigns, expressing the determination and hope that:

> I will cling to the old rugged cross,
> And exchange it some day for a crown.

With *The Presbyterian Hymnal* of 1990, however, hymns expressing that kind of individual, personal piety were much less prominent. Since they are sung by congregations, hymns now are much more likely to use the pronoun "we" rather than "I" or "me." Instead of individually resolving to "cling to the old rugged cross," Presbyterians have been taught by Jane Parker Huber to sing of the rather different relationship to the Savior expressed in "Called as Partners in Christ's Service." Hymns of social service and justice for all have replaced such once-loved songs of personal piety as "The Beautiful Garden of Prayer."

Gone from the hymnal are such hymns as "Onward Christian Soldiers," too militaristic for the post-Vietnam era. Gone, too, are hymns such as "Faith of Our Fathers," deemed gender exclusive. While Presbyterians still sing "In Christ There Is No East or West," those who learned the hymn in their youth are likely to chorus, "Join hands then brothers of the faith," while the rest of the congregation, reading from the new hymnal, are at the same time singing, "Join hands disciples . . . ."

In 1899 the southern Presbyterian Assembly viewed with some alarm a growing tendency on the part of some congregations and stated, "There is no warrant in the Scriptures for the observance of Christmas and Easter as holy days . . . and such observance is contrary to the principles of the Reformed faith." A century later probably a majority of Presbyterian churches were not only observing Christmas and Easter but making use of much of the liturgical year. "The long prayer" of traditional Presbyterianism had been replaced by a number of short prayers, including a prayer of confession followed by an assurance of forgiveness. Little responses punctuated the worship, such as "the Lord be with you" answered by "and also with you." The use of three lectionary readings, usually having little relationship to one another, had replaced the old pattern of reading an Old Testament passage and a New Testament passage dealing in their respective ways with the subject of the sermon.

In 1995 Presbyterians (U.S.A.) and Cumberland Presbyterians published a new *Book of Common Worship.* If you were a Presbyterian time traveler from two centuries earlier now in the twenty-first century worshiping with a congregation using the full service in that book, you might think you were now in an Episcopal church. Leaders of Presbyterian liturgical renewal, however, are quick to point out that many of the prayers of the *Book of Common Worship* are of Presbyterian origin. Through it Presbyterians have discovered the riches both of their own heritage and that of their sisters and brothers in other parts of the story of the one church of Christ.

Presbyterians at Work

If you were a newcomer to a Presbyterian congregation you might be surprised in another way: in a perhaps required orientation class you would be encouraged to become involved in service. On successive Sundays you might hear repeated requests to help in church projects to build a house for the homeless through Habitat for Humanity, take a turn serving in a soup kitchen, donate to a blood drive, share work in a health center, and contribute food and clothes to a thrift store in the inner city. You and your teenagers might be invited to spend a week helping rebuild a church in Appalachia. You might even be challenged to be part of a group visiting a partner church in the Czech Republic or Japan.

When disaster strikes you would know that the Presbyterian Church (U.S.A.) is there with funds and personnel. You would learn about, and through One Great Hour of Sharing contribute to, relief work at home and around the world.

You would also learn that as Presbyterians or in cooperation with other denominations, Presbyterians are at work in mission in almost every country on this globe.

Presbyterians at Prayer

In every age Presbyterians have been a people of prayer. Here are just three examples. President Woodrow Wilson, a devout Presbyterian, wrote this Prayer for Peoples and Rulers:

> Almighty God, Ruler of all peoples of the earth: Forgive, we beseech thee, our shortcomings as a nation; purify our hearts to see and love truth; give wisdom to our counselors and steadfastness to our people; and bring us at last to that fair city of peace whose foundations are mercy, justice, and goodwill, and whose Builder and Maker thou art; through thy Son, Jesus Christ our Lord.[9]

Henry van Dyke (1852–1933) was pastor of a Presbyterian church in New York, a teacher at Princeton Seminary, and a gifted writer. His Prayer for Lent suggests the continuing Calvinistic emphasis on the sinfulness of all of us.

> O merciful Father, who in compassion for thy sinful children didst send thy Son Jesus Christ to be the Saviour of the world: grant us grace to feel and to lament our share in the evil which made it needful for him to suffer and to die for our salvation. Help us by self-denial, prayer, and meditation to prepare our hearts for deeper penitence and a better life. And give us a true

longing to be free from sin, through the deliverance wrought by Jesus Christ, our only Redeemer.[10]

As one looks back over the history of the church, with its sins and schisms, its heroes and heroines, and the blessings God's Spirit has brought the world through the body of Christ, this Prayer for the Mission of the Church, found in the *Book of Common Worship*, seems appropriate:

> Almighty God, you sent your Son Jesus Christ
> to reconcile the world to yourself.
> We praise and bless you
> for those whom you have sent in the power of the Spirit
> to preach the gospel to all nations.
> We thank you that in all parts of the earth
> a community of love has been gathered together
> by their prayers and labors,
> and that in every place your servants call upon your name;
> for the kingdom and the power and the glory
> are yours forever. Amen.[11]

For our continuing story of the church, there can be no ending until the Lord comes again. Instead one must say: "to be continued. . . ."

Questions Chapter 9

1. How did the Presbyterian Church come to America? What can your find out about how your own congregation and your own presbytery were established?
2. Why did Presbyterians not do as well as some others in evangelizing the frontier? What new "frontiers" must Presbyterians reach with the gospel today, and how will we overcome difficulties in reaching these people? What are you doing to help our overseas mission programs?
3. What has caused Presbyterians to divide in the past? How helpful have schisms proved to be? What has helped bring many of us back together again?
4. What changes have you or older members of your congregation seen with regard to Sunday school? worship services? the role of women? other practices?
5. How have our newer confessions come about, and how have they helped express our traditional faith for our new day?
6. As you look back over this whole book, what have been the most interesting and helpful things to you? What has our story suggested we need to do? As the church's story continues, what hope does it give us for the future?

Appendix

Presbyterian Membership in the United States and the World Today

*T*he World Alliance of Reformed Churches Holding to the Presbyterian Form of Government claims a total membership of some 75,000,000 Presbyterians in 107 countries. There are other Presbyterian denominations that do not belong to the World Alliance. There are more Presbyterians in South Korea than in any other nation, and more in Africa than in the United States.

Some "Presbyterian" or "Reformed" Denominations in the United States

The Presbyterian Church (U.S.A.) with some 2,451,654[1] members is the largest Presbyterian denomination in this country. It was formed in 1983 through a merger of northern and southern Presbyterians but traces its ancestry back to early Scotch-Irish immigration.

The Reformed Church in America, the oldest Presbyterian church in America, goes back to 1628 and the Dutch settlement in "New Amsterdam" (later New York). It has often shared in producing educational materials with the Presbyterian Church (U.S.A.) and others. It has about 171,361 members.

The Cumberland Presbyterian Church was formed in 1810 growing out of the Second Great Awakening and protesting the strict Calvinism of early nineteenth-century Presbyterians. It claims about 84,417 members. In 1906 many of the original group reunited with what is now the Presbyterian Church (U.S.A.). For many years it has shared Christian education materials and has cooperated in other ways with the Presbyterian Church (U.S.A.).

The Cumberland Presbyterian Church in America is the sister denomination of the Cumberland Presbyterian Church, with whom it shares a Confession of Faith and Christian education activities. It has about 15,142 mostly African American members.

The United Church of Christ was formed in 1957 from the union of several groups going back to New England's English Puritans (who were Calvinists), German Calvinists, and others. They are sometimes thought of as the most "liberal" of American Reformed churches in theology and social outlook. They claim 1,359,105 members. They often share in producing educational materials with the Presbyterian Church (U.S.A.) and others.

The Presbyterian Church in America was formed in 1973, largely from members of the southern Presbyterian Church who felt that that denomination had become too liberal in theology and social pronouncements. When in 1983 the Presbyterian Church (U.S.A.) was formed, many congregations in the south withdrew, most joining the Presbyterian Church in America. It claims some 254,676 members. It forbids the ordination of women as elders or ministers.

The Christian Reformed Church was formed in 1857 with a base among Dutch immigrants who were arriving in that period. It claims some 137,375 members and is somewhat more conservative than the Reformed Church in America, also of Dutch origin.

The Associate Reformed Presbyterian Church was born in 1782 when two groups that had earlier separated from the Church of Scotland merged in the United States. It has about 35,556 members. It tends to be conservative.

The Evangelical Presbyterian Church was founded in 1981 and seeks to maintain conservative Calvinistic theology. It claims 64,156 members.

The Korean Presbyterian Church, founded in 1976, is made up of some 51,100 members of Korean descent. It cooperates in various ecumenical activities.

The Hungarian Reformed Church in America was formed by immigrants to preserve their heritage from the heroic Hungarian reformers. It has about 6,000 members and is part of the National Council of Churches and the World Alliance of Reformed Churches.

The Orthodox Presbyterian Church was formed in 1936, growing out of the fundamentalist protest that alleged that the Presbyterian Church, U.S.A., now part of the Presbyterian Church (U.S.A.), was too "liberal" in theology and missionary activity. It claims 18,746 members.

The Reformed Presbyterian Church of North America, with 4,363 members, seeks to hold firmly to its roots in the Covenanter movement of the Scottish Reformation.

The Reformed Church in the United States, with 3,258 members, was established in 1725 for German immigrants of the Reformed faith. Many of the original group became part of what is now the United Church of Christ.

For a helpful chart showing Presbyterian divisions and reunions, see the home page of the Presbyterian Historical Society at www.history.pcusa.org. Then click on "Presbyterians in America" and then "Family Tree of Presbyterian Denominations." To shortcut directly to the chart, go to www.history.pcusa .org/pres_hist/family_connections.html.

Notes

CHAPTER 1

1. Tacitus, *Annals,* 15.44, as quoted in *Documents of the Christian Church,* selected and edited by Henry Bettenson (New York: Oxford University Press, 1947), p. 4.

2. See Matthew 10:5–23.

3. See Matthew 18:15–22.

4. Romans 16:15 (New Revised Standard Version). Earlier translations rendered the name as Junius, but subsequent research indicates the feminine form is correct.

CHAPTER 2

1. "The Letter to Diognetus," in *Selections from Early Writers, Illustrative of Church History to the Time of Constantine,* ed. Henry Melvill Gwatkin (London: Macmillan, 1937), pp. 15–17.

2. Justin, *Apology* 67.10–25, in *Selections from Early Writers, Illustrative of Church History to the Time of Constantine,* ed. Henry Melvill Gwatkin (London: Macmillan, 1937), p. 55.

3. As quoted in *Documents of the Christian Church,* ed. Henry Bettenson (New York: Oxford University Press, 1947), pp. 5–6.

4. *The Martyrdom of Perpetua and Felicitas,* as quoted by Justo L. González, *The Story of Christianity,* vol. 1, *The Early Church to the Dawn of the Reformation* (San Francisco: HarperSanFrancisco, 1984), p. 84.

5. As quoted in Bettenson, ed., *Documents,* p. 19.

6. *The Ecclesiastical History of Eusebius Pamphilus* (Grand Rapids: Baker, 1962), 7.15, p. 287. Eusebius's work was probably completed c. AD 340.

7. Ibid., 8.8, p. 327.

8. Ibid., 10.1, pp. 403–4.

9. Ibid., 10.9, p. 439.

10. See Ernest Trice Thompson, *Through the Ages, a History of the Christian Church* (Richmond: CLC Press, 1965). pp. 46–53.

11. Cyprian (c. AD 246), as quoted by John Foster in *Five Minutes a Saint* (Richmond: John Knox, 1963), pp. 16–17.

CHAPTER 3

1. Augustine, *The City of God* 11.1, in *Basic Writings of Saint Augustine,* vol. 2, ed. Whitney H. Oates (New York: Random House, 1948), p. 143.

2. Ibid., 13.14, p. 221.

3. Ibid., 14.3, p. 242.

4. Ibid., 14.13, p. 259.

5. *The Confessions* 1.1, in ibid., vol. 1, p. 3, trans. J. G. Pilkington.

6. Ibid., 2.4, p. 14.

7. Ibid., 8.12, p. 126.

8. *The Call of St. Patrick,* as found in *The Medieval Church,* ed. Roland H. Bainton (Princeton: Van Nostrand, 1962), p. 97.

9. As quoted by Norman F. Langford, *Fire Upon the Earth: The Story of the Christian Church* (Philadelphia: Westminster Press, 1950), p. 68.

10. Ibid., p. 71.

11. The Venerable Bede, *Ecclesiastical History of the English Nation,* as quoted by Ernest Trice Thompson, *Through the Ages: A History of the Christian Church* (Richmond: CLC Press, 1965), p. 107.

12. Ronald H. Bainton, *The Church of Our Fathers* (New York: Charles Scribner's Sons, 1950), p. 100.

CHAPTER 4

1. *The Capture of Jerusalem in 1099,* by Raymond of Agiles, *Historia Francorum,* translated by Frederick Duncalf and August C. Krey, from *Parallel Source Problems in Medieval History,* as found in Roland H. Bainton, *The Medieval Church* (Princeton: Van Nostrand, 1962) p. 119.

2. *Unam Sanctam,* as found in Henry Bettenson, ed., *Documents of the Christian Church* (New York: Oxford University Press, 1947), pp. 161–62.

3. Thomas à Kempis, *The Imitation of Christ* (New York: Grosset & Dunlap, n.d.), chap. I, p. 13.

4. *A Revelation of Love,* chap. 5, as found in *Corpus of Medieval English Prose and Verse,* ed. Marion Glascoe (University of Exeter Press, 1996).

5. The quotations from Hus are as found in Justo L. González, *The Story of Christianity,* vol. 1, *The Early Church to the Dawn of the Reformation* (San Francisco: HarperSanFrancisco, 1984), pp. 350–51.

6. Quoted from *The Chronicle of Daniel Speclin,* in Bainton, *Medieval Church,* p. 187.

CHAPTER 5

1. As quoted by Roland H. Bainton in *The Age of Reformation* (Princeton: Van Nostrand, 1956), p. 28.

2. Ibid., p. 97.

3. Ibid., p. 34.

4. As quoted in Emanuel Stickelberger, *Calvin: A Life,* trans. David Gerog Gelzer (Richmond: John Knox Press, 1954), p. 17.

5. Ibid., p. 148.

6. Ibid., p. 48.

7. Ibid., pp. 56–57.

8. John Christian Wenger, *Even Unto Death: The Heroic Witness of the Sixteenth-Century Anabaptists* (Richmond: John Knox Press, 1961).

9. A fuller transcript of the decrees of the Council of Trent can be found in *Documents of the Christian Church,* ed. Henry Bettenson (New York: Oxford University Press, 1947), pp. 366–74.

10. "From Depths of Woe I Cry to Thee," by Dr. Martin Luther, from *The Handbook to the Lutheran Hymnal* (St. Louis: Concordia, 1942), pp. 234–35, as found on the Internet.

11. From Calvin's commentaries on the Minor Prophets, made available by Shane Rosenthal for *Reformation Link* on the Internet. It is in public domain.

12. As quoted in *In His Likeness*, ed. G. McLeod Bryan (Richmond: John Knox Press, 1959), p. 113.

CHAPTER 6

1. *The Martyrdom of Latimer & Ridley* as found on http:/members.Home.Net/drbrooker/latrid-short.html.

2. As quoted by J. E. Neal in *Queen Elizabeth: A Biography* (Garden City: Doubleday, 1957), p. 58.

3. As quoted by Edmund S. Morgan in *Visible Saints: The History of a Puritan Idea* (New York: New York University Press, 1963), p. 8.

4. As quoted in ibid., pp. 48–49.

5. For more on this group see the next chapter.

6. Edwin Muir, *John Knox: Portrait of a Calvinist* (1929; reprint, Freeport: Books for Libraries Press, 1971), p. 309.

7. A. Mervyn Davies, *Presbyterian Heritage* (Richmond: John Knox Press, 1965), p. 48.

8. As quoted by William M. Ramsay in *The Wall of Separation: A Primer on Church and State* (Louisville: John Knox Press, 1989), pp. 31–32.

9. John Bunyan, *Pilgrim's Progress*, chapter VII, in the University Library of Classics (Books, Inc., 1945) pp. 111–12.

10. As found in the *Book of Confessions* (Louisville: Office of the General Assembly, 1991), 7–1.

CHAPTER 7

1. As quoted by Charles H. Lippy in *Christianity Comes to the Americas 1491–1796* (New York: Paragon House, 1992), p. 293.

2. William Bradford, *History of the Plymouth Plantation,* ch. 4, on the Web at http://members.aol.com/calebj/bradford_journal.html.

3. John Winthrop, *City upon the Hill,* 1630, on the Web at http://www.mtholyoke.edu/acad/intrel/winthrop.htm.

4. As quoted by Dwight A. Randall in "Prayer and Worship" on the Web at http://members.iinet.net.au/~life/prayer_and_worship.html.

5. Richard Hofstadter, *The American Political Tradition and the Men Who Made It* (New York: Random House, 1989), p. 5.

6. Michael Novak, *On Two Wings: Humble Faith and Common Sense at the American Founding* (San Francisco: Encounter Books, 2002).

7. Lord Herbert of Cherbury (d. 1648) is called "the Father of Deism." His "five marks of Deism" may be summarized as follows:

1. A belief in the existence of the Deity
2. The obligation to reverence to such a power
3. The identification of worship with practical morality
4. The obligation to repent of sin and abandon it
5. Divine recompense in this world and the next

8. For a brief statement of the influence of Witherspoon and other Presbyterians on Madison see Gary Willis, *James Madison* (New York: Henry Holt and Company, 2002). Madison was influenced not only by Witherspoon but also by getting to know some Presbyterian ministers.

CHAPTER 8

1. Quoted by William Bean Kennedy in *The Shaping of Protestant Education: An Interpretation of the Sunday School and the Development of Protestant Educational Strategy in the United States, 1780–1860* (New York: Association Press, 1966), pp. 58–59.

2. As quoted by Robert W. Lynn and Elliott Wright in *The Big Little School* (Birmingham: Religious Education Press, 1980), pp. 69–70.

3. Modern History SourceBook: "Sojourner Truth: Ain't I a Woman."

4. Jimmy Carter, *Living Faith* (New York: Random House, 1996), p. 110.

5. As quoted by William M. Ramsay in *Four Modern Prophets: Walter Rauschenbusch, Martin Luther King, Jr., Gustavo Gutiérrez, Rosemary Radford Ruether* (Atlanta: John Knox Press, 1986), p. 82.

6. Reported by Peter Smith in the Louisville *Courier Journal*, June 25, 2001, on the Web at http://www.courier-journal.com/localnews/2001/06/25/ke062501s42424.htm.

CHAPTER 9

1. For this description of mid-eighteenth-century worship I am heavily indebted to an unpublished lecture by Bill Bynam of the Presbyterian Historical Society at Montreat, N.C., delivered there May 29, 2002. Much of the material can be found in Bynam's article, "The Genuine Presbyterian Whine: Presbyterian Worship in the Eighteenth Century," *American Presbyterians: Journal of Presbyterian History* 74 (Fall 1996): 157–70.

2. This is condensed from Smylie's booklet, *A Cloud of Witnesses* (Richmond: CLC Press, 1965), p. 25.

3. *Minutes of the General Assembly of the Presbyterian Church in the United States of America from A.D. 1821 to A.D. 1835 Inclusive* (Philadelphia: Presbyterian Board of Publication, n.d.), p. 378.

4. *The Presbyterian Hymnal* (Philadelphia: Presbyterian Board of Publication, 1874), hymn 885, p. 567.

5. George W. Stroup, *The Promise of Narrative Theology* (Atlanta: John Knox Press, 1981).

6. R. Douglas Brackenridge, *Voice in the Wilderness: A History of the Cumberland Presbyterian Church in Texas* (San Antonio: Trinity University Press, 1968).

7. Ernest Trice Thompson, *Presbyterians in the South,* vol. 2: *1861–1890* (Richmond: John Knox Press, 1973).

8. *The Presbyterian Hymnal* (Philadelphia: Presbyterian Board of Publication, 1874), hymn 765, p. 490.

9. Found in *A Book of Reformed Prayers*, ed. Howard L. Rice and Lamar Williamson Jr. (Louisville: Westminster John Knox Press, 1998), p. 101.

10. Ibid.

11. From the *Book of Common Worship*, prepared by the Theology and Worship Ministry Unit for the Presbyterian Church (U.S.A.) and the Cumberland Presbyterian Church (Louisville: Westminster John Knox Press, 1993), p. 806.

APPENDIX

1. The information concerning dates and membership is derived from *The Yearbook of American and Canadian Churches*, the edition of 2004, Eileen W. Lindner, ed., prepared and edited for the National Council of Churches of Christ in the USA, 475 Riverside Drive, New York, NY 10115-0050, published and distributed by Abingdon Press, Nashville, pages 365–77. The figures are for confirmed members only. The numbers vary from year to year.